Design Thinking

Design Thinking is a set of strategic and creative processes and principles used in the planning and creation of products and solutions to human-centered design problems.

With design and innovation being two key driving principles, this series focuses on, but not limited to, the following areas and topics:

- User Interface (UI) and User Experience (UX) Design

- Psychology of Design

- Human-Computer Interaction (HCI)

- Ergonomic Design

- Product Development and Management

- Virtual and Mixed Reality (VR/XR)

- User-Centered Built Environments and Smart Homes

- Accessibility, Sustainability and Environmental Design

- Learning Design

- Strategy and best practices

This series publishes books aimed at designers, developers, storytellers and problem-solvers in industry to help them understand current developments and best practices at the cutting edge of creativity, to invent new paradigms and solutions, and challenge Creatives to push boundaries to design bigger and better than before.

More information about this series at https://link.springer.com/bookseries/15933

The Art of SXO

Placing UX Design Methods into SEO Best Practices

Zuzanna Krüger

Apress®

The Art of SXO: Placing UX Design Methods into SEO Best Practices

Zuzanna Krüger
Manchester, UK

ISBN-13 (pbk): 978-1-4842-9211-2   ISBN-13 (electronic): 978-1-4842-9212-9
https://doi.org/10.1007/978-1-4842-9212-9

Managing Director, Apress Media LLC: Welmoed Spahr
Acquisitions Editor: James Robinson-Prior
Development Editor: James Markham
Coordinating Editor: Gryffin Winkler

Distributed to the book trade worldwide by Springer Science+Business Media New York, 1 New York Plaza, Suite 4600, New York, NY 10004-1562, USA. Phone 1-800-SPRINGER, fax (201) 348-4505, e-mail orders-ny@springer-sbm.com, or visit www.springeronline.com. Apress Media, LLC is a California LLC and the sole member (owner) is Springer Science + Business Media Finance Inc (SSBM Finance Inc). SSBM Finance Inc is a **Delaware** corporation.

For information on translations, please e-mail booktranslations@springernature.com; for reprint, paperback, or audio rights, please e-mail bookpermissions@springernature.com.

Apress titles may be purchased in bulk for academic, corporate, or promotional use. eBook versions and licenses are also available for most titles. For more information, reference our Print and eBook Bulk Sales web page at http://www.apress.com/bulk-sales.

Any source code or other supplementary material referenced by the author in this book is available to readers on GitHub (github.com/apress). For more detailed information, please visit http://www.apress.com/source-code.

Printed on acid-free paper

*In memory of my sister, a gifted SEO expert,
and my mother, a source of inspiration.*

*To my father, who has been my constant pillar
of strength during these challenging times.*

Table of Contents

About the Author

Zuzanna Krüger is a passionate and innovative SEO professional with a deep understanding of how to effectively drive organic traffic and build sustainable growth strategies. With experience working with clients from around the globe, she has a diverse background in both small businesses and large enterprises and is known for her emphasis on providing real value to customers through her holistic and user-centric approach to website design and optimization. Zuzanna is particularly interested in exploring the potential of AI solutions in the realm of SEO, including natural language processing (NLP) and generative pre-training (GPT). She is constantly seeking out new ways to push the boundaries of what is possible in this rapidly evolving field and is dedicated to helping businesses achieve their full potential through cutting-edge SEO strategies.

About the Technical Reviewer

A senior technical SEO by profession, **Federico Fioravanti**'s core interests are site speed optimization, findability and indexing, site architecture, and on-page technical SEO. He was born and raised in the north of Italy, and after completing his studies, he spent various years between Lisbon (PT) and Budapest (HU) where he currently resides. He has applied experience in online marketing and product management, in particular on projects related to SEO, UX/UI, and front-end design. He has more than eight years of experience in international marketing, working in agile environments and with a strong understanding of industry trends. He is currently a member of an international team made of three senior technical SEO specialists, working closely with stakeholders from different departments on websites with very high organic traffic (33 languages, 50 million users, 200 million monthly organic sessions) and with a technical SEO–reliant architecture. He is also an electronic music composer and an avid photographer who likes taking photos especially while traveling.

Acknowledgments

Writing this book has been a journey filled with love, support, and encouragement from those closest to me. I am deeply grateful to

- My husband Tom, who provided unwavering support, both physical and emotional, throughout the writing process

- My dear friend and colleague Leonardo, who offered invaluable insights on digital marketing and encouraged me to pursue my unconventional projects

- My late mother Magdalena, who always believed in me and cheered me on, even in the most trying times

- My father Jarosław, who constantly encouraged and supported me, giving me the strength to keep going

- My dear grandma Bogna, who always showed enthusiasm for my work, even when it seemed like black magic to her

- And finally, my feline friends and muses Llwynog and Willow, who kept me entertained and motivated when the writing was tough

I am humbled and grateful for the love and support of each and every one of you.

Introduction

Many companies have forgotten they sell to actual people. Humans care about the entire experience, not just the marketing or sales or service. To really win in the modern age, you must solve for humans.[1]

—Dharmesh Shah, CTO and Cofounder, HubSpot

As the world of digital marketing continues to evolve, so too must the way we think about optimizing our websites for search engine visibility and conversion. With the latest algorithm updates from Google and other major search engines, it's become increasingly clear that the traditional methods of SEO (search engine optimization) design are no longer enough to guarantee success online.

Instead, a new approach is needed that takes into account the latest changes in how search engines operate and how users interact with websites. First and foremost, we must consider the needs of the user and design our websites with their entire search journey in mind. This means taking a holistic approach that combines the disciplines of SEO, CRO (conversion rate optimization), and UX (user experience) design to provide a smooth browsing experience that leads users from a search engine all the way through to your checkout page. This approach is known as search experience optimization, or SXO for short.

---

[1] Haden, J. (2013). How to Sell to Humans. [online] Inc.com. Available at www.inc.com/magazine/201311/jeff-haden/hubspot-co-founder-says-inbound-marketing-is-not-the-answer.html [Accessed Feb. 19, 2023].

What Is SXO?

In essence, SXO is a new emerging field that combines the disciplines of SEO, CRO, and UX, offering a comprehensive approach to website optimization. Unlike traditional SEO, which is focused primarily on ranking in search engine results pages (SERPs), SXO is focused on creating a positive browsing experience for users at every stage of their interaction with your website—from the initial search query all the way through to the checkout page.

In order to achieve this, SXO must be considered at every stage of the website design process, from the initial keyword research right through to the final user testing. This requires a thorough understanding of the user's journey from start to finish and designing every element of the website accordingly. It also implies using data and experimentation to constantly improve the user experience.

In short, SXO is all about putting the user first and creating a search *experience* that is both informative and enjoyable.

Who Is This Book For?

While the concept of SXO is still fairly new, there are a number of experts who are already using this approach to great effect. In this book, we will draw on the collective experience of some of the world's leading marketing experts to provide readers with a comprehensive guide to SXO. We will cover everything from the basics of SXO to more advanced tactics, making this the perfect resource for anyone looking to get the most out of their search traffic.

So, whether you're a business owner looking to grow your revenue from organic traffic, an SEO professional wanting to learn about SXO, or a CRO specialist or UX designer wanting to utilize organic traffic to create high-converting user journeys, this book will give you the tools and knowledge you need to succeed.

CHAPTER 1

Search Experience Optimization: The New Way to Do SEO

As mentioned in the Introduction, SXO is a new approach to website optimization that combines the disciplines of SEO, CRO, and UX design. In this chapter, we will take a more in-depth look at what SXO entails, its main components, and the theory behind it.

The Three Pillars of SXO

The foundation of SXO is built on three pillars: SEO, CRO, and UX design. In order to understand SXO properly, it's important to have a basic understanding of each of these disciplines. Figure shows them in more detail.

Z. Krüger, *The Art of SXO*, Design Thinking, https://doi.org/10.1007/978-1-4842-9212-9_1

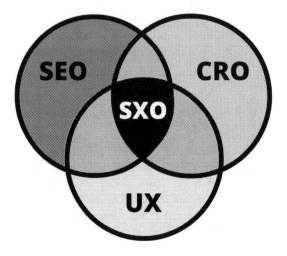

SEO

Search engine optimization (SEO) is the process of optimizing a website for Google and other major search engines. The goal of SEO is to improve the visibility of a website in organic (nonpaid) search results, with the ultimate aim of driving more traffic to the site.

There are two main types of SEO: on-page SEO and off-page SEO. On-page SEO refers to the optimization of a website's content and code, in order to make it more accessible and relevant to search engines. This includes optimizing titles, descriptions, and keyword usage. Off-page SEO, on the other hand, refers to all SEO tactics that don't involve working with the content within a website. This includes link building, brand building, citation building, content marketing, and social media, all of which aim to help both search engines and users understand the website better and increase its authority, trust, and relevance.

In recent years, there has been a shift away from traditional SEO techniques such as keyword stuffing[1] and link buying.[2] These days, Google's algorithms are much more sophisticated and are designed to penalize[3] sites that engage in black hat[4] practices. Instead, the focus is on creating high-quality content that is relevant and useful to users.[5]

CRO

Conversion rate optimization (CRO) is the process of optimizing a website with the goal of increasing the percentage of visitors who take a desired action. This could be anything from making a purchase to signing up for a newsletter or downloading a PDF.

---

[1] Keyword stuffing is a black hat SEO technique that involves overusing certain keywords or phrases in an attempt to manipulate a search engine's algorithm and achieve a higher ranking for a particular page. This technique used to be somewhat effective in the early days of search engines, when they were primarily keyword based, but search engines have become much more sophisticated in recent years and can now detect and penalize keyword stuffing.

[2] Link buying involves purchasing links from other websites in order to artificially boost the search engine ranking of a website. The purchased links may be irrelevant to the content of the website and are often placed on low-quality, spammy websites. This technique is in violation of Google's Webmaster Guidelines and can result in a penalty or even a complete removal from search engine results pages (SERPs).

[3] A penalty from Google drastically lowers a website's organic visibility as a result of violating Google's Webmaster Guidelines. A penalty can range from a drop in ranking for a few specific keywords to a complete removal from search engine results. There are many types of penalties, such as a manual penalty imposed by a Google employee or an algorithmic penalty imposed automatically by Google's search algorithm.

[4] Black hat describes techniques that violate search engine guidelines and attempt to manipulate search engine results. Black hat techniques are unethical and can harm both the website's ranking and visibility. In contrast, white hat techniques adhere to search engine guidelines and aim to provide the best user experience possible.

[5] Google has stated on multiple occasions that creating great content is one of the most important things a website can do to improve its search engine ranking. For more information, visit developers.google.com/search/docs/fundamentals/creating-helpful-content.

CRO is usually accomplished through A/B testing, which involves showing two different versions of a web page to two groups of users ("A" and "B"). The version that performs better in terms of the desired conversion rate is then used as the new standard.

CRO can be used to test anything from the copy on a web page to the design, layout, and even the location of elements. By constantly testing and improving your website's conversion rate, you can significantly increase your revenue without necessarily driving more traffic to the site.

UX Design

User experience (UX) design is the process of designing websites and applications with the goal of providing a positive and enjoyable experience for users. This includes everything from the overall look and feel of a site to how easy it is to navigate and use.

Good UX design is essential for keeping visitors on your site and ensuring that they have a positive experience. It's also been shown to improve conversion rates, as users are more likely to take the desired action when they enjoy using your site.

The User-First Approach

All three of these disciplines (SEO, CRO, and UX design) share a common goal: to improve the experience of users on your website. This is what sets SXO apart from traditional SEO, which often focuses on game-playing search engine algorithms instead of actual users.

The user-first approach of SXO means that everything you do should be aimed at improving the experience of users on your site. This includes creating high-quality and useful content, making it easy for users to find what they're looking for, and ensuring that the overall design of your site is pleasing to the eye.

Let's say, for example, that you want to increase the number of visitors to your site who take the desired action. In order to do this, you need to first understand what users want and need from your site. Once you know this, you can make the necessary changes to your content, design, and code to make it more user-friendly and thus more likely to convert.

The user-first approach is not only more effective, but it's also more sustainable in the long run. By focusing on providing a positive experience for users, you're more likely to build a loyal following that will continue to use your site even as algorithms change.

What are the key components of the user-first approach?

Creating Content for Users

One of the most important aspects of SXO is creating content that is informative and helpful to users. This means writing articles, blog posts, and even product descriptions with the user in mind, rather than trying to game the system with keyword-stuffed content.

Let's take a look at an example.

Suppose you run an ecommerce website selling men's shoes. Your goal is to increase the number of visitors to your site and convert more of them into paying customers.

To do this, you could focus on creating keyword-rich content that ranks highly in Google search results and stuff your text with several long-tail keywords[6] that are easy to rank for, for example, black leather men's shoes size 10 or elegant men's shoes carbon fiber. However, if the content is not

---

[6] Long-tail keywords are more specific and less commonly used keyword phrases that typically consist of three or more words. They are used to target niche audiences and increase the chances of ranking for a particular search query. Because long-tail keywords are more specific, they generally have less competition and can result in higher click-through rates (CTR) and conversion rates. In contrast, short-tail keywords are broader and more general and typically have more competition and lower conversion rates.

relevant or useful to users and it's long and difficult to read due to too many oddly placed synonyms, they're likely to click back to the search results page and continue looking for a better option. In this case, you've wasted your time and effort creating content that doesn't actually help you achieve your goal.

Instead, it would be more effective to focus on creating helpful and informative product descriptions that make it easy for users to browse and skim through the most important details to find the right shoes for them. In addition, include images and videos that show the shoes in use so users can get a better idea of what they look like and how they might fit. By creating content with the user experience in mind, you're more likely to keep visitors on your site and increase the chances of them making a purchase.

The goal is to create content that is so useful and relevant that users will want to share it with their friends and followers. This not only helps to improve your SEO, but it also helps to build trust and credibility with your audience.

The most efficient way to create content for users is to focus on solving their problems. This could be anything from teaching them how to do something to providing information that they're looking for. Once you know what kinds of problems your users are trying to solve, you can create content that addresses those needs.

To find out what problems your users are trying to solve, you can use a variety of methods, such as

- Asking them directly through surveys or polls

- Reviewing customer service logs to see what questions people are asking

- Checking social media platforms like Twitter and Facebook to see what people are saying about your industry

- Using Google Ads[7] to see what keywords people are searching for related to your business

Once you know what problems your users are trying to solve, you can create content that addresses those needs. For example, if you run a website selling products for dogs, you could create blog posts with titles such as "5 Ways to Keep Your Dog Entertained During Winter" or "How to Choose the Right Dog Food for Your Pet." By creating content that helps users solve their problems, you're more likely to keep them engaged with your site.

Making Information Easily Accessible

In addition to creating helpful content, it's also important to make sure that information is easy for users to find. This means structuring your website in a way that is logical and easy to navigate.

One way to do this is to use a clear and consistent hierarchy on your website. This means organizing your pages in a way that reflects the importance of the information. For instance, if you have a page about your company's history, it would make sense to place it under the "About Us" section.

---

[7] Google Ads is an online advertising platform developed by Google, where businesses can create and display ads to users who are searching for specific keywords or visiting specific websites. The platform uses a pay-per-click (PPC) model, where advertisers only pay when someone clicks on their ad. Advertisers can create different types of ads, including text ads, display ads, video ads, and shopping ads, and can target specific audiences based on factors such as location, interests, and behavior. Google Ads can be a powerful tool for businesses to reach potential customers and increase their online visibility.

It's also important to use clear and descriptive titles for your pages and blog posts. This makes it easier for users to find the information they're looking for, and it also helps search engines index your site more effectively. For example, instead of titling a blog post "5 Tips for Choosing the Right Dog Food," it would be more effective to title it "How to Choose the Right Dog Food for Your Pet."

In addition to using clear titles, you should also use descriptive headings and subheadings throughout your content. This makes it easier for users to skim through and find the most relevant information.

Finally, you should also include links to related content throughout your site. This helps users find additional information that they might be interested in, and it also helps to improve your SEO. For example, if you have a blog post about choosing the right dog food, you could include links to your company's page about dog food.

By making information easily accessible, you're more likely to keep users engaged with your site.

Creating a Pleasant Design

Creating helpful and easy-to-find content is important, but it's also essential to make sure that your website is pleasant to look at. This means using a clean and consistent design that is easy on the eyes.

There are a few key elements to creating a pleasant design, such as

- Use of whitespace: Using long walls of text on a page can be overwhelming for users. To make your pages more readable, you should break long paragraphs into sections, lists, and tables—all separated by ample whitespace.

- Use of color: Using color effectively can help to create a more pleasant design. You should use colors that complement each other and make sure that there is enough contrast between the text and the background.

- Use of images: Adding images to your pages can help to break up the text and make your site more visually appealing. However, you should only use images that are relevant to the content and add value for users.

- Use of fonts: When it comes to choosing a font for your website, readability should be a top priority. Sans-serif fonts such as Arial, Verdana, and Helvetica are generally considered to be the easiest to read on digital screens.[8] It's also important to consider the size of the font, as both too small and too large text can cause strain on readers' eyes. Google recommends using a minimum font size of 16px for body text,[9] as this size provides a good balance between readability and the amount of content that can fit on the screen.

---

[8] Sans-serif fonts are typefaces that do not have the small lines or flourishes at the ends of letters, known as serifs. Sans-serif fonts are often considered more modern and minimalistic in appearance and are commonly used in digital media, such as websites and mobile apps. Serif fonts, on the other hand, do have the small lines or serifs at the ends of letters. Serif fonts are often associated with traditional printed materials, such as books and newspapers. However, it doesn't mean that choosing a serif font for your website is always a bad choice. Different font styles can evoke different emotions and associations in users. For example, sans-serif fonts may be perceived as more modern and minimalistic, while serif fonts may be perceived as more traditional and trustworthy.

[9] For the type scale of other elements, visit m2.material.io/design/typography/the-type-system.html#type-scale.

Another important aspect of design is usability. If your site is difficult to use, chances are good that users will give up and go elsewhere.[10]

Some common usability issues include

- Confusing navigation

- Hard-to-read text

- Small buttons or links

- Pop-ups and other intrusive ads

All of these things can make it difficult for users to use your site, which is why it's important to avoid them.

In addition to these technical aspects, it's also important to create a site that feels welcoming. This means using language that is friendly and easy to understand. It also means avoiding anything that could come across as pushy or salesy. Your website should be a reflection of your company, so make sure that it conveys the same values and message.

By creating a site that is pleasant to look at and easy to use, you're more likely to keep users engaged.

Key Takeaways

The user-first approach is all about creating a website that is designed with the user in mind. This means creating helpful and easy-to-find content, using a clean and consistent design, and making sure that your site is easy to use. By putting the user first, you're more likely to create a successful website that users will want to come back to.

---

[10] A study by Google found that 79% of users will leave a site and look for another option if they don't find what they're looking for or if the site is too difficult to use. This shows that usability is a key factor in determining whether or not users will stay on a website. (Source: thinkwithgoogle.com/marketing-resources/data-measurement/mobile-page-speed-new-industry-benchmarks/.)

Some key takeaways from this section include

- It's important to create helpful and easy-to-find content. This means using clear titles and descriptive headings, as well as including links to related content.

- Your website should have a clean and consistent design. This means maintaining an optimum level of whitespace in the design composition, using colors that complement each other, and using images that add value for users.

- Your site should be easy to use. This means avoiding anything that could make it difficult for users to navigate or find the information they're looking for.

- Remember to put the user first. This means creating a site that is designed with the user in mind. By doing this, you're more likely to create a successful website.

By following these guidelines, you can create a website that is both search engine- and user-friendly, which will help you to improve your search rankings and grow your business.

The Power of Data

In order to create a successful website, it's important to use data. Data can help you understand how users are interacting with your site and what they're looking for. This information can then be used to improve the user experience and make sure that your site is meeting their needs.

Introduction to Data

If you want to be successful with SXO, it's important to have a strong understanding of data. Data can help you understand how visitors are interacting with your site, what they're looking for, and what they're interested in.

There are a number of data types that are important to SXO, including

- Website data

- Search data

- User data

Website data includes things like pageviews, bounce rate, and time on site. This type of data can help you understand how visitors are interacting with your site.

Search data includes things like keyword rankings and organic traffic. This type of data can help you understand what people are searching for and how well your site is ranking for those keywords.

User data includes things like age, location, and gender. This type of data can help you understand who your audience is and what they're interested in.

All of these types of data are important to consider when optimizing your website. By understanding how visitors are interacting with your site, you can make changes to improve the experience.

Collecting Data

Collecting data is the first step to understanding your visitors. There are a number of ways to collect data, including

- Using web analytics tools

- Conducting user research

- Setting up conversion tracking

- Using heatmaps

- A/B testing

Web analytics tools, such as Google Analytics, can give you a wealth of data about your website. These tools can track things like pageviews, time on site, and bounce rate. This data can be helpful in understanding how visitors are interacting with your site.

Conducting user research can also be helpful in understanding your audience. This can be done through surveys, interviews, or focus groups. This type of research can help you understand things like what people are looking for on your site and what their pain points are.

Setting up conversion tracking is also important if you want to understand how effective your site is at converting visitors into customers or subscribers. This can be done through tools like Google Analytics or Crazy Egg. By tracking conversions, you can understand which areas of your site are working well and which need improvement.

Heatmaps are another helpful tool in understanding how visitors are interacting with your site. Heatmaps track things like where people are clicking and how far they scroll down the page. This data can be helpful in understanding what people are interested in and where they're getting stuck.

A/B testing is also a helpful way to collect data. This involves showing two different versions of your site to users and then measuring which one performs better. This can be helpful in understanding what changes to make to improve the user experience.

Analyzing Data

Once you've collected data, it's important to analyze it to see what it's telling you. This involves looking for patterns and trends and then trying to understand what they mean.

For example, if you see that your website's bounce rate is high, this could be an indication that something is wrong with the site. Maybe the design is confusing, or the content is not relevant to what people are looking for.

If you see that your organic traffic is increasing, this could be an indication that your SXO efforts are paying off. It could also be a sign that you're ranking for more keywords or that your site is being shared more often.

Data analysis is an important part of understanding your website's performance. By understanding what the data is telling you, you can make changes to improve your site.

The Importance of Data Interpretation

It's important to remember that data is only helpful if you can interpret it correctly. Just because you see a pattern in the data doesn't mean that it's accurate. There could be other factors at play that you're not considering.

For example, let's say you see a sharp decrease in your website's traffic. This could be caused by a number of things, such as a change in your ranking or a decrease in the number of people searching for your keywords. It could also be caused by something unrelated to your website, like a change in the seasonality of searches.

It's important to consider all of the factors that could be affecting the data before you make any decisions. Otherwise, you could make changes that don't actually improve your website.

But how do you ensure that you're interpreting the data correctly?

One approach is to use multiple data sources. For example, if you're trying to understand why your traffic is down, you could look at your website's analytics, as well as your search engine rankings. This would give you a more complete picture of what's going on and would help you to make more informed decisions.

Another approach is to use data from multiple time periods. For instance, you could compare your current traffic levels to those from a month ago or a year ago. This would help you to see if the decrease is part of a larger trend or if it's an isolated incident.

Lastly, it's important to talk to other people about the data. This could be your team or other people in your industry. By talking to others, you can get different perspectives on the data, and this can help you to understand it better.

Data Visualization Techniques

Once you've collected and interpreted your data, it's important to visualize it in a way that's easy to understand. This is where data visualization comes in.

There are a number of different data visualization techniques that you can use, and the best one for you will depend on the type of data you're working with and what you're trying to achieve.

Some common data visualization techniques include

- Bar charts

- Line graphs

- Pie charts

- Maps

- Tables

Each of these techniques has its own strengths and weaknesses, so it's important to choose the right one for your needs.

For example, bar charts are great for comparing data points, but they don't show changes over time very well. Line graphs, on the other hand, are great for showing trends over time. Pie charts are good for showing proportions, but they can be difficult to interpret if there are too many data points.

Once you've chosen a data visualization technique, it's important to make sure that the visualization is easy to understand. This means using clear and concise labels and choosing colors that are easy to distinguish.

It's also important to make sure that the visualization is accurate. This means double-checking your calculations and using a tool like Excel to create the visualization.

Creating an effective data visualization can be a challenge, but it's worth taking the time to do it right. A well-designed visualization can be very helpful in understanding your data and making better decisions for your website.

Making Decisions Based on Data

Once you've collected and interpreted your data, it's time to make some decisions.

This can be a difficult process, as you need to weigh up all of the different factors that are affecting your website. However, there are some general guidelines that you can follow to make sure that you're making the best decisions for your website.

One of the most important things to remember is that you can't make decisions based on a single data point. It's important to look at all of the data and to understand how it fits together.

Another important thing to remember is that data can be misleading. This is why it's so important to interpret the data correctly and to understand what it's telling you.

For example, if you're looking at your website's traffic, it's important to understand where the traffic is coming from. If most of your traffic is coming from a single source, then that source could be skewing your data.

It's also important to remember that data changes over time. This means that you need to regularly check your data and make sure that you're making decisions based on the most up-to-date information.

What are some of the most important things to remember when making decisions based on data?

1. *You can't make decisions based on a single data point.*

2. *Data can be misleading.*

3. *Data changes over time.*

4. *You need to understand what the data is telling you.*

5. *You need to make sure that you're making decisions based on the most up-to-date information.*

Making decisions based on data can be difficult, but it's important to remember that data is a valuable tool. Used correctly, it can help you to make better decisions for your website and to improve your website's performance.

Implementing Changes Based on Data

Once you've made some decisions about your website, it's time to implement those changes. This can be a difficult process, as you need to make sure that the changes you're making are effective and that they don't cause any problems for your website.

There are a few things to keep in mind when implementing changes to your website.

First, it's important to make sure that you're making small, incremental changes. This will help you to avoid any major problems and will make it easier to track the results of your changes.

Second, it's important to test your changes before you implement them. This means creating a test website or using a tool like Google Optimize to test how your changes will affect your traffic.

Third, it's important to monitor the results of your changes. This means regularly checking your data and making sure that your changes are having the desired effect. If they're not, then you can make further changes or revert back to the original version of your website.

What are some of the most important things to keep in mind when implementing changes to your website?

1. *Make small, incremental changes.*

2. *Test your changes before you implement them.*

3. *Monitor the results of your changes.*

4. *Be prepared to make further changes if necessary.*

Introducing changes on your website can be a challenge, but it's important to remember these guidelines. By following these guidelines, you can be sure that you're making effective changes that won't cause any problems for your website.

Key Takeaways

In this section, we've looked at some of the most important things to remember when making decisions about your website. Here are the key takeaways from this section:

- Data is a valuable tool that can help you to make better decisions for your website.

- There are a number of ways to collect data, including web analytics tools, A/B testing, and surveys.

- You need to make sure that you're making decisions based on the most up-to-date information.

- When implementing changes to your website, it's important to make small, incremental changes.

- You should test your changes before you implement them.

- Monitor the results of your changes, and be prepared to make further changes if necessary.

By following these guidelines, you can be sure that you're making the best decisions for your website and that you're implementing effective changes that won't cause any problems for your website.

The Importance of Design

Design is an important part of SXO. It's not enough to just optimize your website for search engines and conversions; you also need to make sure that it looks good and provides a positive user experience. Good design can help you to improve your website's SXO, while bad design can hurt it.

In this section, we'll talk about the importance of design and how you can incorporate it into your SXO strategy. We'll also discuss the principles of good design and how you can create a good design for your site.

The Role of Design in SXO

There are a few reasons why design is an essential part of an effective SXO strategy.

User Experience

As we mentioned before, good design will improve the user experience of your site. This is important because it can encourage visitors to stay on your site and convert them into customers or subscribers.

Let's take a look at an example. Imagine that you're looking for a new pair of shoes. You find a website that has a lot of shoes to choose from, but the site is difficult to navigate. The shoes are arranged in random order, and it's hard to find the size and style that you're looking for. After a few minutes of frustration, you give up and leave the site.

Now, imagine that you find another website that sells shoes. The site is well-designed, and it's easy to find the size and style that you're looking for. There aren't as many shoes to choose from, but you're able to find the perfect pair quickly and easily. You make your purchase, and you're happy with the experience.

Which site are you more likely to visit again in the future? Which site would you recommend to a friend? The answer is obvious. Good design has a positive impact on user engagement and retention.

Search Engine Rankings

Good design can also impact your search engine rankings. Google's algorithms take into account the design of your site when determining your rankings.[11] This means that a good design can help you to improve your search engine rankings and to get more traffic to your site.

---

[11] In general, Google's algorithm considers a wide range of factors when ranking websites, including relevance, authority, mobile-friendliness, page speed, and user experience. Good design can contribute to a positive user experience and help to make a website more appealing and easy to navigate, which can in turn improve user engagement and reduce bounce rates. These factors may indirectly impact a website's search engine ranking, as Google's algorithm considers user engagement and other metrics as important signals for ranking.

There are a few factors that Google looks at when determining the design of your site. These include

- The layout of your site
- The use of whitespace
- The font size and style
- The color scheme
- The imagery
- The overall user experience

Let's take a look at an example. Imagine that you have two websites, and both websites sell shoes. Website A has a well-designed layout, with a clear navigation system and easy-to-read text. Website B is cramped and cluttered, with a confusing navigation system and small, hard-to-read text. Which website do you think Google is going to rank higher?

The answer is website A. Google wants to provide its users with the best possible experience, and that means returning results from websites that are well-designed and easy to use.

Brand Reputation

Good design can also help to build trust with your visitors. Have you ever been to a website that looked like it was made in the 1990s? If so, you probably didn't stay for long. On the other hand, have you ever been to a website that looked modern and professional? If so, you were probably more likely to trust the site and to consider making a purchase.

People are naturally distrustful of businesses that don't invest in their online presence. A well-designed website shows visitors that you're a professional, credible business.

Good design is essential for an effective SXO strategy. But it's important to remember that design isn't just about how your website looks. Design is also about how your website works. In the next section, we'll take a look at the principles of good design and how you can create a good design for your site.

The Principles of Good Design

There are a few principles that all good designs share. These principles include

- Simplicity

- Consistency

- Clarity

- A focus on the user

Simplicity

The best designs are often the simplest ones. This doesn't mean that your design should be boring or basic. It just means that your design should be easy to understand and use.

When it comes to simplicity, less is almost always more. This is especially true when it comes to the use of whitespace. Whitespace is the empty space around the elements on your page. It's important to use whitespace in your design, as it can help to make your page more readable and easy to navigate.

Consistency

Consistency is another important principle of good design. This means using similar colors, fonts, and styles throughout your website. This helps to create a cohesive look, and it makes your site easier to navigate.

It's important to be consistent with the overall look and feel of your site. But you also need to be consistent with the user experience. This means using the same navigation system on every page of your site and making sure that all of your links work correctly.

Clarity

Clarity is another essential principle of good design. This means making sure that your text is easy to read and that your website is easy to understand.

One way to achieve this is to use headings and subheadings. This helps to break up your text and to make it easier to scan. It's also important to use clear and concise language. Avoid using technical jargon, unless you're sure that your audience will understand it.

A Focus on the User

The final principle of good design is a focus on the user. This means creating a website that is easy to use and that meets the needs of your target audience.

It's important to think about who your target audience is and what they need from your website. For example, if you're targeting a mature audience, you'll need to make sure that your website is easy to use. This might mean using larger fonts and avoiding complicated navigation.

If you're targeting a younger audience, on the other hand, you might want to focus on creating a more engaging design. This could include adding images and videos and using bolder colors.

Remember, your goal is to create a design that meets the needs of your target audience. By doing this, you'll be more likely to create a successful website.

Creating a Good Design for Your Website

Now that we've looked at the principles of good design, let's take a look at how you can create a good design for your website.

There are a few things that you need to consider when creating your design. These include the following.

Your Industry and Market

The first thing you need to consider when creating your design is your industry and market. You need to understand the trends in your industry and what your competitors are doing. This will help you to create a design that is unique and that will stand out from the crowd.

The Message You Want to Communicate

The next thing you need to consider is the message you want to communicate. What do you want your website to say about your brand? What are your goals for your website? Once you know this, you can start to create a design that reflects your message.

Your Target Audience

As we mentioned before, it's important to think about who your target audience is when creating your design. You need to consider their needs and what they're looking for from your website. By understanding your target audience, you can create a design that appeals to them.

Data from Your Analytics

Finally, you need to consider the data from your analytics. This includes things like the average time spent on your website, the bounce rate, and the most popular pages. This data will help you to understand how people are using your website and what needs to be improved.

By considering all of these factors, you can create a good design for your website. Remember, your goal is to create a design that is appealing to your target audience and that helps you to achieve your goals.

Applying the Design Principles

Now that we've looked at the principles of good design, let's take a look at how you can apply them to your own website in a few easy steps.

Use Typography to Create a Hierarchy of Information

One way to apply the principle of hierarchy is to use typography. This means using different font sizes, and bold or italic text, to create a hierarchy of information. By doing this, you can ensure that the most important information is easy to see.

Use Whitespace to Create Visual Interest

Another way to apply the principle of whitespace is to use it to create visual interest. You can do this by adding margins and padding to your design. This will help to break up your text and to make your website more visually appealing.

Use Color to Create Contrast

You can also use color to create contrast. This means using two or more colors that are different, but that work well together. For example, you could use a light color for your background and a dark color for your text. This will help to make your text easier to read.

Use Imagery to Add Visual Interest

Finally, you can use imagery to add visual interest. This includes adding photos, illustrations, and videos to your website. By doing this, you can make your website more visually appealing and help to break up your text.

By applying the principles of good design, you can create a website that is easy to use and that meets the needs of your target audience.

Designing for Different Devices

It's important to remember that people will be accessing your website from a variety of different devices. This includes desktop computers, laptops, tablets, and smartphones.

There are a few things you need to consider when creating a responsive design.

The Layout of Your Website

When creating the layout for your website, you need to think about how it will look on different screen sizes. You should avoid using fixed widths and instead use percentages or fluid grids.[12] This will help to ensure that your website looks good on all screen sizes.

---

[12] A fluid grid is a web design technique that involves using relative units (such as percentages) to size elements on a web page, instead of fixed units (such as pixels). This allows the design to be more flexible and adapt to different screen sizes and devices, from desktops to smartphones. A well-designed fluid grid can help to create a consistent and cohesive visual experience across different devices and ensure that the content is easily readable and accessible.

The Size of Your Text

You also need to consider the size of your text. This is particularly important for mobile devices. You should use a large, easy-to-read font size for your text.

The Size of Your Images

Finally, you need to consider the size of your images. When using images on your website, you should use responsive images. This means using images that are automatically resized to fit the screen they're being viewed on.

By considering all of these factors, you can create a responsive design that looks good on all devices.

Key Takeaways

In this section, we've looked at the principles of good design. We've also looked at how you can apply these principles to your own website. Remember, your goal is to create a website that

- Makes it easy for visitors to navigate your site: This includes using a clear navigation system and adding links to relevant pages, which will make your information structure easy to understand and follow for both real users and search engine bots.

- Meets the needs of your target audience: This includes considering who your target audience is and what they're looking for on your website.

- Serves information in an easy-to-digest format: This includes using typography, whitespace, and color to create a hierarchy of information and adding imagery to add visual interest.

- Creates a positive first impression: This includes ensuring that your website looks professional and builds trust.

- Is designed for different devices: This includes creating a responsive design that looks good and loads fast on all screen sizes, reducing the amount of scrolling and clicking required, and reducing the amount of data that needs to be downloaded.

By following these tips, you can create a website that is appealing to both users and search engines.

The Role of Content

In this section, we're going to look at the role of content in SXO. We'll start by looking at what content is and what it's used for. We'll then look at the different types of content that you can use on your website.

What Is Content?

Content is the information on your website that helps visitors to understand what your website is about. Content can take many different forms, including text, images, videos, and infographics.

Content serves several different purposes:

- It helps visitors to understand what your website is about.

- It helps search engines to understand what your website is about and to index your website correctly.

- It can help to improve your website's conversion rate by providing visitors with information that they're looking for.

- It can help to build trust with your visitors by providing accurate and reliable information.

- It can be used to promote your brand, products, or services.

Without good quality content, it will be difficult to achieve success with your SXO efforts. How do you create good quality content? In the next section, we'll look at some tips for creating content that is both informative and engaging depending on the industry/vertical in which you're working.

The Different Types of Content

When creating content for your website, there are several things that you should keep in mind:

- The needs of your target audience: What information are they looking for?

- The goals of your website: What do you want visitors to do on your website?

- The tone of voice of your website: What is the overall tone or voice that you want to use on your website?

- The format of your content: How do you want to present the information on your website?

- The length of your content: How long should each piece of content be?

- The frequency of your content: How often should you add new content to your website?

- The keyword density of your content: How many keywords should you use in each piece of content?

Based on these factors, there are several different types of content that you can use on your website:

- Text-based content: This is the most common type of content and includes articles, blog posts, product descriptions, and FAQs.

- Visual content: This includes images, infographics, and videos.

- Interactive content: This includes quizzes, surveys, and polls.

- User-generated content: This includes reviews, testimonials, and comments.

Text-based content is the most common type of content because it's relatively easy to create and can be used to target a wide range of keywords. However, visual content can be very effective at grabbing attention and promoting your brand. Interactive content can be used to engage visitors and get them involved with your website. User-generated content can help to build trust and credibility and can also be used to target long-tail keywords.

You can also classify content based on its purpose:

- Informational content: This includes articles, blog posts, tutorials, and FAQs. Its purpose is to educate the reader and provide them with information that they're looking for.

- Promotional content: This includes product descriptions, sales pages, and banner ads. Its purpose is to promote your products or services.

- Branding content: This includes your website's design, logo, and tagline. Its purpose is to build trust and credibility and to promote your brand.

Different types of content will be more effective at different stages of the customer journey. For example, informational content is most effective at the top of the funnel, when visitors are just beginning their research. Promotional content is most effective at the bottom of the funnel, when visitors are ready to buy. Branding content is important throughout the entire customer journey, in order to build trust and credibility with your visitors.

Now that you know what content is and what it's used for, let's look at some tips for creating good quality content.

Creating High-Quality Content

Creating great content isn't easy, but it's definitely worth the effort. High-quality content will help you to rank higher in search results, improve your conversion rate, and build trust and credibility with your target audience.

Before you start creating content, you need to know who your target audience is and what they're looking for. Once you know this, you can create content that is relevant to their needs and interests.

Your content should also be well-written, engaging, and informative. It should be free of grammar and spelling errors and should flow smoothly from one sentence to the next.

In order to make your content more engaging, you can use images, infographics, and videos. You can also use headings and subheadings to break up your text and make it easier to read.

Finally, your content should be keyword-rich. This means including words and phrases related to your topic that people may search for in order to find content like yours. Including these keywords helps search engines identify what the content is about, making it easier for users to discover. You should also use relevant terms throughout the text so readers can understand the context of what they are reading. This will help them better understand the content and the associated topic or concept. However, you should be careful not to overuse keywords, or else your content may sound unnatural and be difficult to read.

Creating high-quality content takes time and effort, but it's definitely worth it. To make it easier, you can use this checklist that covers the most important points:

- Who is your target audience?

- What are they looking for?

- Is your content relevant to their needs and interests?

- Is your content well-written, engaging, and informative?

- Does it flow smoothly from one sentence to the next?

- Do you use headings and subheadings to break up your text?

- Do you use images, infographics, and videos to make your content more engaging?

- Is your content keyword-rich?

- Are you careful not to overuse keywords?

If you can answer yes to all of these questions, then you're well on your way to creating high-quality content.

Key Takeaways

In this section, you learned about the different types of content and what they're used for. You also learned about some tips for creating high-quality content. Remember to keep these points in mind when creating content for your website:

- Always know who your target audience is and what they're looking for.

- Create content that is relevant to their needs and interests.

- Make sure your content is well-written, engaging, and informative.

- Use headings and subheadings to break up your text.

- Use images, infographics, and videos to make your content more engaging.

- Include relevant keywords throughout your text.

If you follow these tips, you'll be on your way to creating high-quality content that will help you to improve your search ranking, increase your conversion rate, and build trust and credibility with your target audience.

The Science of a Good Browsing Experience

How Search Engines Work

Search engines are designed to help users find the information they're looking for. To do this, they use a number of different algorithms to crawl[13] (scan) the Internet and index websites.

When a user types a query into a search engine, the search engine looks through its index to find the websites and pages that are relevant to the query. The search engine then ranks these results in order of relevance and displays them to the user.

The ranking of results is determined by a number of factors, including the quality of the content, the relevancy of the keywords used, and the popularity of the website.

In order to ensure that your website is found by search engines and ranked highly in results pages, you need to make sure that your website is optimized for search engines.

Meeting Expectations

When a user types a query into a search engine, they have a specific goal or need in mind. This is known as user intent.

There are a number of different types of user intent, and it's important to understand which type of intent your target audience has when they're searching for keywords related to your business.

---

[13] Crawl refers to the process of search engines like Google scanning a website and collecting information about its pages and content. During a crawl, search engine bots visit a website's pages and follow links to other pages on the site, indexing the content as they go. The information collected during a crawl is used to create the search engine's index, which is then used to determine search results. Website owners can use a robots.txt file to control which pages on their site are crawled by search engines and which are not.

34

There are four main types of intent:

- Navigational: The user is looking for a specific website or page.

- Informational: The user is looking for information on a topic.

- Transactional: The user is looking to buy a product or service.

- Commercial: The user is looking for a coupon or discount.

Depending on the type of intent, the user will be at different stages of the marketing funnel. It's important to understand where your target audience is in the marketing funnel so that you can create content that is relevant to their needs.

For example:

- If your target audience has navigational intent, they are likely looking for your website specifically. In this case, you need to make sure that your website is easy to find and navigate.

- If your target audience has informational intent, they are likely looking for information on a topic related to your business. In this case, you need to create high-quality content that is relevant to their needs.

- If your target audience has transactional intent, they are likely looking to buy a product or service from you. In this case, you need to make sure that your website is designed for conversion and that your offer is attractive.

- If your target audience has commercial intent, they are likely browsing and comparing different products or services before making a purchase. In this case, you need to make sure that your prices are competitive and that you are offering a competitive deal.

Being Found

There are a number of different techniques that you can use to optimize your website for search engines. These include using the right keywords, creating high-quality content, and building links to your website. However, there is no one silver bullet when it comes to SEO. The best way to increase your chances of being found by search engines is to diversify your strategy.

Let's have a look at the factors that search engines typically use to rank websites:

- The quality of the website's content: This is one of the most important ranking factors. Search engines want to provide users with high-quality, relevant results. Therefore, it's important to create content that is well-written, informative, and relevant to your target audience.

- Use of keywords: Keywords are still an important factor in ranking, but they need to be used in a way that is natural and not forced. Stuffing your content with keywords will not only turn off readers, but it will also likely result in a penalty from Google.

- Links to your website: Links are still an important ranking factor. Search engines use links as a way to measure the popularity and authority of your website. The more high-quality links you have pointing to your site, the better your chances of ranking well.

- The loading speed of your website: Website speed is now an official ranking factor for both desktop and mobile searches. In addition to being ranked lower, slow websites can also frustrate users, which may lead to them leaving without taking any action.

- User experience: User experience is becoming increasingly important as a ranking factor. This includes factors such as the design of your website, how easy it is to navigate, and whether or not users are able to find what they're looking for.

There are a number of other factors that can influence your ranking, but these are some of the most important ones. Now let's take a look at the categories of different techniques SEO specialists use to increase their chances of ranking:

- On-page SEO: On-page SEO is the process of optimizing your website's pages for search engines. This includes factors such as choosing the right keywords, creating well-written and informative content, and making sure your website's design is user-friendly.

- Off-page SEO: Off-page SEO is the process of optimizing your website for factors that are not controlled by you. This includes building links to your website, creating social media profiles, and being active on forums and in other online communities.

- Technical SEO: Technical SEO is the process of making sure your website's technical aspects are optimized for search engines. This includes things like website speed, sitemaps, and redirects.

- Local SEO: Local SEO is the process of optimizing your website for local search results. This includes things like claiming your business listing on directories, creating location-specific pages, and building links from local websites.

- Mobile SEO: Mobile SEO is the process of optimizing your website for mobile devices. This includes things like creating a mobile-friendly design, using responsive design, and improving website speed.

- International SEO: International SEO is the process of optimizing your website for search engines in multiple countries and languages. This includes things like targeting the right keywords and optimizing website content for different languages and regions, as well as implementing hreflang tags and managing international domains.

SEO is an ever-evolving process, and there are always new techniques and strategies that you can learn. The best way to stay up to date on the latest SEO news is to follow SEO blogs and forums. Some of the best ones include Moz, Search Engine Land, and Google Webmaster Central Blog.

Serving Information

Users should be able to find the information they need quickly and easily. This means that the content must be well-organized, using headings, lists, and other formatting techniques to make it easy to scan. The language should be clear and concise, without any jargon. And the overall tone should be engaging and interesting.

The most effective information structure is one that is hierarchical, with the most important information at the top and the less important information further down. This is how most websites are structured, using a hierarchy of pages and subpages.

But, in SXO, in order to get users to the most important information as quickly as possible, you can use several techniques that go beyond the traditional hierarchical structure:

1. Landing pages: A landing page is a stand-alone page that is designed to get users to take a specific action. Landing pages are often used in online marketing campaigns, and they usually have a very clear and concise message.

2. Microsites: A microsite is a small website that is typically used for a specific marketing campaign or product launch. Microsites are usually separate from the main website, and they often have their own domain name.

3. Single pages: A single page is a web page that contains all of the information about a specific topic on one page. Single pages are often used for topics that are time-sensitive, such as news stories or event listings.

4. Widgets: A widget is a small piece of code that can be added to a website to display dynamic content. Widgets are often used to add social media feeds, weather forecasts, or other types of content that changes frequently.

5. Content silos: A content silo is a group of related content that is organized in a way that makes it easy for users to find what they're looking for. Content silos are often used on ecommerce websites, with each product category being its own content silo.

6. Content pillar: A content pillar is a single, comprehensive piece of content that covers everything there is to know about a particular topic. Content pillars are often used in blog posts and articles, and they are a great way to build authority on a topic.

7. FAQs: A FAQ is a list of questions and answers that are relevant to a particular topic. FAQs are often used to provide information about products, services, or policies.

8. How-tos: A how-to is a step-by-step guide that shows users how to do something. How-tos are often used to provide instructions for using a product or service, and they can be a great way to build trust with your audience.

9. Glossaries: A glossary is a list of terms and their definitions. Glossaries are often used to provide clarification on technical or specialized topics.

10. Case studies: A case study is an in-depth look at how a particular company or organization has used a product or service to achieve their goals. Case studies are a great way to show potential customers how your product or service can be used in the real world.

The goal of SXO is to make it as easy as possible for users to find the information they need. By using techniques like landing pages, microsites, single pages, widgets, and content silos, we can help users get to the information they need quickly and easily. And by creating content pillars, FAQs, how-tos, glossaries, and case studies, you can provide them with the comprehensive information they need to make a decision.

Providing Solutions

The goal of SXO is to make it as easy as possible for users to find the information they need and convert them into customers. In order to do this, we need to understand how people make decisions.

People are always looking for ways to save time and effort. When they're trying to make a decision, they're looking for the quickest and easiest way to get the information they need. They don't want to have to wade through a bunch of information that's not relevant to their needs.

This is why it's so important to have a well-organized website. If your website is easy to navigate, users will be able to find the information they need quickly and easily. On the other hand, if your website is cluttered and confusing, users will likely give up and go elsewhere.

In addition to making it easy for users to find the information they need, you also need to provide them with the information they need to make a decision. This means having well-written and informative content. If your content is full of fluff and empty promises, users will see right through it and move on.

Finally, you need to provide a sense of urgency. People are more likely to make a decision if they feel like they need to act quickly. This could be in the form of a sale that's about to end or an offer that's only available for a limited time.

Most people think that the decision-making process is rational and logical. But, in reality, the decision-making process is often emotional and irrational.

There are two types of decision-makers, those who make decisions based on logic and those who make decisions based on emotion:

- Logical decision-makers base their decisions on facts and data. They want to know all the details before they make a decision.

- Emotional decision-makers base their decisions on their gut feeling. They are more likely to make a decision quickly, without gathering all of the information.

Most people are a mix of both logical and emotional decision-makers. But, in general, people tend to favor one type over the other.

So, how do you appeal to both types of decision-makers?

The key is to provide both logic and emotion:

- If you're targeting logical decision-makers, your content should be focused on facts and data. You should provide detailed information about your product or service, and you should use statistics and case studies to support your claims.

- If you're targeting emotional decision-makers, your content should be focused on creating positive feelings and emotions. You should use images, stories, and testimonials to connect with your audience on an emotional level.

No matter what type of decision-maker you're targeting, it's important to remember that people want solutions to their problems. SXO is all about providing solutions to users' needs.

By understanding the psychology of decision-making, we can create content that appeals to the needs of our target audience and convert them into customers.

Building Loyalty

The goal of SXO is not only to get users to convert into customers but also to create loyalty and turn them into brand advocates. When people are loyal to a brand, they're more likely to buy from that brand again in the future. They're also more likely to recommend the brand to their friends and family.

But before you can create loyalty, you need to establish yourself as an authority in your industry and build trust with your audience.

There are a few ways to do this:

- Use statistics and data: Statistics and data help to build trust and credibility. They show that you know what you're talking about and that you're not making false claims.

- Use social proof: Social proof is when people see others using your product or service, and they want to use it too. You can use testimonials, reviews, and social media to create social proof.

- Be transparent: Transparency builds trust by showing people that you have nothing to hide. Be open about your business practices, your policies, and your team.

- Be a thought leader: Position yourself as an expert in your industry by writing blog posts, speaking at conferences, and being active on social media.

- Offer a guarantee: Offering a money-back guarantee shows people that you're confident in your product or service and that you're willing to stand behind it.

By establishing yourself as an authority and building trust with your audience, you can nurture loyalty and turn them into brand advocates. There are a few key things you can do to achieve it:

1. Make it easy for customers to buy from you: The easier it is for them to buy, the more likely they are to buy from you again in the future.

2. Provide excellent customer service: If you provide good customer service, people will be more likely to buy from you again and recommend you to their friends.

3. Offer loyalty programs: Loyalty programs give customers an incentive to keep coming back. They also make people feel like they're part of a community or a VIP.

4. Say "thank you": Showing appreciation goes a long way toward creating loyalty. A simple "thank you" can make someone feel appreciated and valued, and it can encourage them to do business with you again in the future.

The goal of SXO is not only to get users to convert into customers but also to create loyalty and turn them into brand advocates. You can accomplish a lot if you establish yourself as an expert and develop trust with your audience. If you make it easy for customers to buy from you and show appreciation, you can easily turn them into paying customers.

Key Takeaways

- Search engines work by crawling the Internet and indexing the content found on websites.

- In order to be found online, your website needs to be well-optimized for search engines. This means matching the user's intent, using the right keywords, and building backlinks to your website.

- You can present information in a number of ways, but the most important thing is to make sure it's easy to read and understand. Use short paragraphs, headings, and lists to break up the text, and use images and graphs to illustrate your points.

- SXO is not only about getting users to convert into customers but also about creating loyalty and turning them into brand advocates. You can accomplish this by establishing yourself as an authority and building trust with your audience.

Summary

- Search experience optimization (SXO) is a new emerging field that combines the disciplines of SEO, CRO, and UX design to create websites that are not only optimized for search engines but also highly effective at converting visitors into customers or subscribers.

- SXO is based on the user-first approach, which means that website designers and marketers should focus on creating websites that are easy to use and provide a great user experience.

- Website owners should track data about their website visitors in order to understand their needs and interests. They can then use this data to create content and design features that will appeal to their target audience.

- The role of design in SXO is to help website designers understand how users interact with their websites and what they're looking for.

- The role of content in SXO is to provide users with the information they need in a format that is easy to consume and understand.

- The goal of SXO is not only to get users to convert into customers but also to create loyalty and turn them into brand advocates.

CHAPTER 2

Applying SXO to Your Website

Now that we've covered the basics of SXO, it's time to apply it to your own website. In this chapter, we'll walk you through the process of conducting a search experience audit, defining your business goals, and identifying your target audience. We'll also cover the basics of keyword research and website structure. By the end of this chapter, you'll have a solid plan for improving your website's search experience.

Understanding Your Website's Current Search Experience

The first step in applying SXO to your website is understanding your site's current search experience. This means taking a look at how users are currently finding and interacting with your site through search engines. This will help you to understand where your website is currently falling short and what areas need improvement.

There are a few key factors you'll want to consider when conducting your audit:

- Search engine visibility: How easy can potential customers find your website when they search for relevant keywords?

© Zuzanna Krüger 2023
Z. Krüger, *The Art of SXO*, Design Thinking, https://doi.org/10.1007/978-1-4842-9212-9_2

- Keyword targeting: Are you targeting the right keywords? Are you using those keywords effectively on your website?

- Website structure: Is your website easy to navigate? Are your pages well-organized and relevant to your target keywords?

- Content: Is your content relevant to your target keywords? Is it well-written and engaging?

- Design: Is your website's design user-friendly and visually appealing?

- Conversions: Are visitors to your website taking the desired actions?

Once you've identified the areas that need improvement, you can start to develop a plan for how to optimize your website.

To get started, you'll first need to choose the right tools and gather data. There are a number of tools you can use to conduct your search experience audit:

- Google Analytics: Provides data and insights on user behavior, acquisition, and conversions on your website. You can view information about how users are interacting with your site, including the number of sessions, pageviews, bounce rate, and more. You can also use Google Analytics to track your marketing campaigns, create custom reports, and set up goals to measure the success of your site.

- Google Search Console: Monitors your website's search performance, alerts you to critical errors, and provides insights to optimize your site's visibility in search results. With Search Console, you can see which keywords are driving traffic to your site, monitor your site's health, and ensure that Google can access your site's content. You can also use Search Console to submit sitemaps, request indexing, and view search analytics data.

- Screaming Frog: Crawls your website to analyze on-page elements, identify technical issues, and provide recommendations for optimization. This tool allows you to quickly identify problems such as broken links, missing meta descriptions, duplicate content, and more. You can also use Screaming Frog to extract data, audit redirects, and analyze page titles and descriptions.

- Microsoft Clarity: Offers heatmaps and session replays to help you visualize user behavior and identify opportunities to optimize their experience. With Clarity, you can see where users are clicking, how far they are scrolling, and where they are dropping off. You can also filter the data to analyze specific segments of users and view session replays to get a more detailed understanding of user behavior.

- Google Spreadsheets: Helps you organize, analyze, and visualize your website's data for ongoing tracking and performance measurement. With this tool, you can create custom reports and dashboards, as well as analyze large sets of data with pivot tables and charts. You can also use Google Spreadsheets to collaborate with others and share your data easily.

- Google Looker Studio: Lets you create interactive, shareable dashboards and reports to help you better understand your website's data and make informed decisions. Looker Studio offers a range of visualization options, including bar charts, line graphs, and pie charts, and allows you to customize the layout and style of your reports. You can also use Looker Studio to connect to various data sources and automate data refreshes.

- Google PageSpeed Insights: Measures your website's performance on both mobile and desktop devices and provides actionable suggestions to improve page speed and user experience. With PageSpeed Insights, you can identify and prioritize opportunities to optimize your site's speed, including compressing images, minimizing render-blocking resources, and improving server response time.

- Google Tag Manager: Enables you to manage and deploy marketing and analytics tags on your website without requiring coding skills. This tool allows you to add and update tags easily, as well as test and debug tags before publishing. You can also use Google Tag Manager to control when and where tags fire and to integrate with other Google tools such as Analytics and Ads.

- Google Keyword Planner: Offers data and suggestions on keyword ideas, search volume, and competition to help you optimize your website's content for search engines. With Keyword Planner, you can search for new keyword ideas, get historical statistics on keywords, and view forecasts for potential traffic. You can also use Keyword Planner to analyze your competition and create ad campaigns.

Gathering Data with Google Analytics

Once you've chosen the right tools, it's time to start gathering data. First, you'll want to take a look at your website's traffic data. This will help you to understand how users are currently finding and interacting with your site.

Google Analytics is a great tool for this. It can show you things like

- The number of users who visit your site

- How they found your site (e.g., through a search engine, social media, direct traffic, etc.)

- What pages they visit

- How long they spend on each page

- What actions they take on your site (e.g., sign up for a newsletter, make a purchase, etc.)

1. Setting Up Your Google Analytics Account

If you don't already have a Google Analytics account, you'll need to set one up. This is a quick and easy process that only requires a few minutes of your time. You can do this on google.com/analytics.

Once you're on the site, click "Sign In" in the top right-hand corner. You'll be taken to a page where you can either sign in with your existing Google account or create a new one.

From there, click "Access Analytics," which will take you to the Google Analytics terms of service page. Once you've read and agreed to the terms, click "I Accept."

You'll then be taken to the "Create an Account" page, where you'll need to enter some basic information about your website. This includes things like your website's name, URL, and time zone.

Once you've entered all of the required information, click "Create." You'll then be given your tracking code, which you'll need to add to your website.

2. Adding Your Google Analytics Tracking Code

Once you have your tracking code, you'll need to add it to your website. There are three ways to do this:

- Adding the code to your CMS: If you're using a content management system (CMS) like WordPress or Squarespace, there are plug-ins or modules that can be used to add your tracking code to your website.

- Adding the code to your hosting account: Some hosting providers allow you to add your tracking code directly to your account. This is usually done through a control panel or administrative dashboard.

- Adding the code manually: If you're not using a CMS or your hosting provider doesn't offer this option, you'll need to add the code manually. To do this, you'll need to edit your website's HTML code.

If you need to add the code manually, you can do so in two ways: through Google Tag Manager or by adding the code directly to your website. We recommend the first option, as it's much easier to do and offers more flexibility.

A. Adding the Code Through Google Tag Manager

If you're not familiar with Google Tag Manager, it's a free tool that allows you to manage your website's tags (including tracking codes) in one place. This makes it much easier to add, remove, and change your website's tags.

To get started, go to tagmanager.google.com and click "Create Account." You'll then be asked to enter some basic information about your account, such as your name and website URL.

Once you've entered all the required information, click "Continue." You'll then be given your tracking code, which you'll need to add to your website either by using one of the preceding options or manually.

B. Adding the Code Directly to Your Website

If you choose to add the code directly to your website, you'll need to edit your website's HTML code. To do this, you'll need to use a text editor like Notepad++ or Sublime Text.

How to access your website's code will depend on what kind of website you have. If you're using a CMS like WordPress, you can access your code through the "Editor" section of your dashboard.

If you're not using a CMS, you'll need to download your website's files from your server and edit them locally on your computer, for example, by using an FTP client like FileZilla.

Once you have access to your website's code, you'll need to locate the <head> section. This is where you'll add your tracking code.

Your tracking code should look something like this:

```
<!-- Google Analytics Tracking Code -->
<script>(function(i,s,o,g,r,a,m){i['GoogleAnalytics
Object']=r;i[r]=i[r]||function(){ (i[r].q=i[r].q||[]).
push(arguments)},i[r].l=1*new Date();a=s.createElement(o),
m=s.getElementsByTagName(o)[0];a.async=1;a.src=g;m.parentNode.
```

```
insertBefore(a,m) })(window,document,'script','//www.google-
analytics.com/analytics.js','ga'); ga('create', 'UA-xxxxxx-1',
'auto'); ga('send', 'pageview');</script>
```

There, UA-xxxxxx-1 should be replaced with your own Google Analytics tracking code that you can find in your Analytics account by going to Admin ➤ View Settings.

Once you've added your tracking code, save your changes and upload the edited file(s) back to your server. Your Google Analytics tracking code should now be active, and you'll start collecting data about your website's traffic.

3. Viewing Your Data in Google Analytics

A. The Basics

Once you've added your tracking code and started collecting data, it's time to take a look at what Analytics can tell you about your website's traffic.

To do this, log in to your Analytics account and click "Reporting" in the sidebar. You'll then be taken to the "Standard Reporting" page, which gives you an overview of how your website is performing.

The first thing you'll see is the "Audience Overview" report, which gives you a general overview of your website's traffic.

This report includes information such as

- The number of sessions (visits) over a given period of time

- The number of users (unique visitors) over a given period of time

- The number of pageviews over a given period of time

- The average session duration

- The bounce rate

You can use this report to get a general idea of how your website is performing. If you want to dig deeper, you can click any of the links in the sidebar to view more detailed reports.

For example, the "Acquisition" section contains reports that tell you where your traffic is coming from, such as organic search, paid search, social media, etc.

The "Behavior" section contains reports that tell you what people do on your website, such as which pages they visit, how long they spend on each page, etc.

The "Conversions" section contains reports that tell you how well your website is performing in terms of goals, such as sales, leads, sign-ups, etc.

Google Analytics also offers a number of other features that can be useful for understanding your website's traffic. For example, you can use the "Segments" feature to create custom groups of users and then view reports for just those groups.

You can also use the "Custom Reports" feature to create your own reports with the specific data that you want to see.

And if you ever need help understanding something in Google Analytics, you can always check out the "Help" section in the sidebar. I also recommend checking out Google's Analytics Academy, which offers free courses on how to use Analytics.

B. Using Google Analytics to Track Your Goals

One of the most important things you can do with Google Analytics is to track your website's goals.

A goal is any action that you want your users to take on your website, such as making a purchase, signing up for a newsletter, filling out a form, etc.

By tracking goals, you can see which parts of your website are doing well in terms of conversion rate (the percentage of people who take the desired action) and which parts need improvement.

To track goals in Google Analytics, go to the "Admin" section and click "Goals" in the "View" column.

On the "Goals" page, you'll see a list of any goals that you've already set up. To add a new goal, click the "New Goal" button.

You'll then be taken to the "Goal Setup" page, where you'll need to enter some information about your goal.

First, you'll need to give your goal a name and choose a "Goal Type." There are four types of goals in Google Analytics:

- Destination: A destination goal is triggered when someone arrives at a specific page on your website, such as a thank-you page after filling out a form.

- Duration: A duration goal is triggered when someone spends a certain amount of time on your website.

- Pages/Screens per session: A pages/screens per session goal is triggered when someone views a certain number of pages or screens on your website.

- Event: An event goal is triggered when someone performs a specific action on your website, such as clicking a button or link.

After you've chosen a goal type, you'll need to enter the necessary information for that goal type.

For example, if you're tracking a destination goal, you'll need to enter the URL of the thank-you page.

If you're tracking an event goal, you'll need to enter the category, action, and label for that event.

Once you've entered all of the necessary information for your goal, click the "Save" button.

You can then view your goals in the "Reporting" section. To do this, go to the "Standard Reporting" tab and click "Goals" in the sidebar.

On the "Goals" page, you'll see a list of all of your goals and some important metrics for each goal, such as conversion rate and revenue.

You can also click any of the goals to get more detailed reports.

Example goals you should consider tracking:

- Number of people who sign up for your newsletter

- Number of people who fill out a contact form

- Number of people who make a purchase

- Number of people who download a whitepaper or ebook

- Number of people who watch a video

- Number of people who click a link to a landing page

- Number of people who click an ad

- Number of people who spend a certain amount of time on your website

- Number of people who view a certain number of pages on your website

C. Using Google Analytics to Track Your Traffic Sources

It's also important to track where your website's traffic is coming from.

There are a number of different traffic sources, such as organic search, direct traffic, referral traffic, social media traffic, and paid traffic.

Each traffic source has its own set of benefits and drawbacks, so it's important to track how each one is performing in terms of conversion rate and revenue.

To track your website's traffic sources, go to the "Acquisition" tab in the sidebar and click "All Traffic" in the drop-down menu.

On the "All Traffic" page, you'll see a list of all of your website's traffic sources and some important metrics for each one, such as conversion rate and revenue.

You can also click any of the traffic sources to get more detailed reports.

Some things you should consider when looking at your website's traffic sources:

- Which traffic sources are sending the most visitors to your website?

- Which traffic sources have the highest conversion rates?

- Which traffic sources have the lowest conversion rates?

- Which traffic sources generate the most revenue?

- Which traffic sources generate the least amount of revenue?

D. Using Google Analytics to Track Your Website's Performance

It's also important to track how well your website is performing in terms of pageviews, unique visitors, bounce rate, and average time on site.

To track your website's performance, go to the "Audience" tab in the sidebar and click "Overview" in the drop-down menu.

On the "Overview" page, you'll see a number of important metrics, such as pageviews, unique visitors, bounce rate, and average time on site.

You can also click any of the metrics to get more detailed reports.

Some things you should consider when looking at your website's performance:

- How many pageviews does your website get?

- How many unique visitors does your website get?

- What is your website's bounce rate?

- What is the average time spent on your website?

- Are there any pages on your website that have a high bounce rate or low average time spent?

E. Creating Custom Reports in Google Analytics

Google Analytics comes with a number of prebuilt reports that you can use to track your website's traffic, goals, and other data: Website Overview report, Acquisition report, Behavior report, and Conversion report.

However, you can also create your own custom reports. This can be useful if you want to track specific data that isn't already being tracked by a prebuilt report.

To create a custom report:

1. Go to the "Customization" tab in the sidebar and click "New Custom Report" in the drop-down menu.

2. On the "New Custom Report" page, you'll need to give your report a name and description.

3. You'll also need to select the type of report you want to create. There are four types of reports: Explorer, Flat Table, Pie Chart, and Bar Chart.

4. Once you've selected the type of report you want to create, you'll need to add a metric and a dimension.

   a. A metric is a piece of data that you want to track, such as pageviews or unique visitors.

   b. A dimension is a way of categorizing your data, such as browser or traffic source.

5. Once you've added all the metrics and dimensions
    you want to track, click "Save" to create your report.

You can now view your report by going to the "Customization" tab and clicking the report you just created.

Gathering Data with Google Search Console

Google Search Console is a free tool that can be used to track your website's performance in search results. It also provides data on the keywords that are driving traffic to your site, as well as the click-through rate (CTR) and position of your site for those keywords. This data can be extremely valuable when you're trying to improve your website's search ranking.

1. Setting Up Your Google Search Console Account

To get started with Google Search Console, you'll need to add your website to the tool and verify that you're the owner of the site.

Once you've verified your website, you can start tracking your data. Some things you should track in Google Search Console:

- The keywords that are driving traffic to your site

- The CTR of your site for those keywords

- The position of your site for those keywords

- Any errors that are preventing your site from appearing in search results

2. Viewing Your Data in Google Search Console

To view your data in Google Search Console, go to the "Performance" tab in the sidebar.

On the "Performance" page, you'll see a number of important metrics, such as

- Clicks: The number of times your site has been clicked in search results

- Impressions: The number of times your site has appeared in search results

- CTR: The percentage of people who click your site in search results

- Average position: The average position of your site in search results

You can also click any of the metrics to get more detailed reports. Some things you should consider when looking at your website's performance:

- How many clicks is your website getting?

- How many impressions is your website getting?

- What is your website's CTR?

- What is your website's average position?

- Are there any keywords that have a low CTR or high average position?

3. Using Google Spreadsheets or Microsoft Excel to Find Key Information

If you want to read information from Google Search Console more efficiently, you can use a spreadsheet program like Google Spreadsheets or Microsoft Excel to use advanced formulas and calculate data and present it visually.

To get started, you'll need to export your data from Google Search Console into a CSV file.

Once you have your CSV file, you can open it in a spreadsheet program like Google Spreadsheets or Microsoft Excel. You can also use add-ons such as SEO Tools for Excel (seotoolsforexcel.com) or Search Analytics for Spreadsheets (searchanalyticsforsheets.com).

Once you have your data in a spreadsheet, you can start playing around with it and manipulating it to find the information you're looking for, such as

- The average CTR for your website

- The average position of your website

- The number of clicks you got for a certain keyword

- The number of impressions you got for a certain keyword

- Find underperforming pages or keywords

For example, let's say you want to find the keywords that have the highest CTR.

You can do this by sorting your data by CTR in descending order. This will give you a list of the keywords with the highest CTR at the top.

You can also use formulas to calculate things like average CTR or position. For example, the following formula is one I use on a daily basis:

```
=arrayformula((if(F2:F<=10,if(E2:E<3%,"Improve meta",(if(F2:F<>
"",if(F2:F>5,if(F2:F<20,"Improve content",""),""),"")))," "")))
```

This formula will mark any page that could be quickly SEO-optimized by either improving its contents or metadata.

Gathering Data with Microsoft Clarity

Microsoft Clarity is a free analytics tool that provides insights into user behavior on your website. Clarity can help you understand what people are doing on your website, where they're getting stuck, and how to improve your user's experience.

1. Setting Up Your Microsoft Clarity Account

To get started with Microsoft Clarity, you'll need to sign up for a free account and add the Clarity tracking code to your website. The process is nearly identical to installing the Google Analytics tag on your website—you can either use the manual method or the Google Tag Manager method.

Once you've done that, Clarity will start collecting data about your website's visitors.

Some of the things you can track with Clarity include

- Clicks

- Hover events

- Scroll depth

- Input field interactions

- Session recordings

2. Viewing Your Data in Microsoft Clarity

Once you've been collecting data for a while, you can start to see some patterns emerge. For example, you might notice that a lot of people are clicking on a certain part of your website or that they're having trouble filling out a form.

Start by looking at your data in the Clarity dashboard. The dashboard gives you an overview of your website's performance, including how many people are visiting, how long they're staying, and what pages they're looking at.

You can also view heatmaps and session recordings in Clarity. Heatmaps show you where people are clicking on your website, and session recordings let you see what people are doing on your website in real time. These can be really helpful in understanding how people are interacting with your website and where they're having trouble.

3. Filtering Data in Microsoft Clarity

One of the most powerful features of Clarity is the ability to filter your data. For example, you can look at only people who came to your website from a certain source or only people who clicked a certain link.

You can also segment your data by device type, browser, and operating system. This can be helpful in understanding how people are interacting with your website on different devices and browsers.

For example, you might notice that people are having trouble filling out a form on your website when they're using a mobile device. Or you might notice that people using a certain browser are more likely to click a certain link.

4. Creating Reports in Microsoft Clarity

Once you've found some interesting patterns in your data, you can create a report to share with others. Reports can be really helpful in getting buy-in from stakeholders or decision-makers.

To create a report, click the "Reports" tab in the Clarity dashboard and then click "Create Report."

You'll be able to select which metric you want to track and which time period you want to include. You can also add a title and description to your report.

Once you're happy with your report, click "Share" to generate a link that you can send to others.

Gathering Data with Screaming Frog

Screaming Frog is a website crawler that can be used to gather data about your website. It's a really useful tool for understanding how search engines see your website and for finding issues that need to be fixed. It's the only paid tool on this list, but it's worth the price for the amount of data it can collect. It's also quite affordable, at only $149 per year. However, if your website has less than 500 pages, you can use the free version.

1. Installing and Configuring Screaming Frog

To get started with Screaming Frog, you'll need to download and install the program. Once it's installed, open the program and click "Configuration" ➤ "Spider."

On the Spider Configuration page, you'll need to enter your website's URL. You can also specify which types of files you want to crawl and how many threads you want to use.

If you're not sure what settings to use, you can leave the defaults. Here are the typical settings I use to run my audits:

- Follow Internal "nofollow[1]": This will tell the crawler to follow links even if they're marked as "nofollow."

---

[1] Nofollow is an HTML attribute that can be added to a link to tell search engines not to pass PageRank or other link equity to the linked page. The nofollow attribute is typically used on links that are sponsored, paid, or user-generated and which the website owner doesn't want to be seen as endorsing. By using the nofollow attribute, website owners can avoid penalties from Google for violating Google's Webmaster Guidelines on link schemes.

- Crawl Canonicals:[2] This allows us to crawl canonical link elements.

- Crawl Next/Prev: This allows us to crawl rel="next" and rel="prev" properties to better understand paginated content.

- Crawl Linked XML Sitemaps:[3] This will crawl any linked XML sitemaps.

- Auto Discover XML Sitemaps via robots.txt:[4] This will automatically discover XML sitemaps via your website's robots.txt file.

---

[2] A canonical URL is the preferred URL for a piece of content, which is used to avoid duplicate content issues and to help search engines understand which version of the content to index. When there are multiple versions of the same content available at different URLs, search engines may be unsure which one to show in their search results. By using a canonical tag in the HTML header of a page, website owners can signal to search engines that a particular URL should be considered the canonical or preferred version of the content. This can help to consolidate link equity and ensure that the correct version of the content is displayed in search results.

[3] An XML sitemap is a file that lists all the pages of a website and provides metadata about each page such as the last time it was updated and how frequently it changes. XML sitemaps are used by search engines to more effectively crawl and index a website's pages, as they provide a complete and organized view of a site's structure. By submitting an XML sitemap to search engines like Google, website owners can help to ensure that all their important pages are crawled and indexed.

[4] Robots.txt is a text file that can be placed in the root directory of a website, which gives instructions to search engine bots on which pages to crawl and which to exclude. The file contains a set of directives, such as User-agent and Disallow, which tell search engines which pages or directories they should not crawl. The robots.txt file is used to help search engines better understand a website's structure and content and can be an important tool for controlling how a website appears in search results. It's important to note, however, that the robots.txt file is simply a set of guidelines, and search engines may still crawl and index pages that are excluded if they find links to them elsewhere on the Web.

2. Crawling Your Website with Screaming Frog

Once you've configured the settings, click "Start" to begin crawling your website. Depending on the size of your website, this could take a few minutes or a few hours. Screaming Frog will go through your website and collect data about each page, including the title, metadata, headers, and more. It will also look for broken links and other errors.

Once the crawl is complete, you'll see a list of all the pages on your website, along with some data about each page.

You can also connect Screaming Frog to Google Analytics, Search Console, PageSpeed Insights, and other apps to collect even more data. To do this, click "Configuration" ➤ "API Access" and select the app you want to connect to.

3. Analyzing Your Data in Screaming Frog

Once the crawl is complete, you can begin analyzing your data. There are a few different ways to do this:

- First, you can use the "Bulk Export" feature to export all of your data into a spreadsheet. This is useful if you want to analyze your data in more detail or if you want to share it with someone else. To do this, click "Bulk Export" ➤ "All Results."

- You can also use the "Filters" feature to find specific types of pages or issues. For example, you can filter for 404 errors or for pages with missing title tags. To do this, click "Filters" ➤ "Add."

- Finally, you can use the "Reports" feature to generate reports about your data. These reports can be really helpful in getting buy-in from stakeholders or decision-makers. To create a report, click "Reports" ➤ "Create Report." You'll be able to select which metric you want to track and which time period you want to include. You can also add a title and description to your report. Once you're happy with your report, click "Generate Report" to generate it.

Since Screaming Frog can be quite technical, in this guide we'll focus on analyzing the exported data in Google Spreadsheets and Looker Studio which are much more beginner-friendly. However, if you'd like to learn more about using Screaming Frog, I'd recommend checking out their documentation.

Analyzing Data with Google Spreadsheets

There are countless ways to analyze your exported data with Google Spreadsheets. In this section, we'll focus on a few key aspects most important for SXO.

1. Identifying Pages with Missing Meta Descriptions and Title Tags

To do this, we're going to use the export from Screaming Frog and the "Filter" function in Google Spreadsheets.

1. First, open your exported Screaming Frog data in Google Spreadsheets. Then, click "Data" ➤ "Filter." This will add a filter to your data.

2. Next, click the arrow next to the "Meta Description" column and select "(blank)." This will filter for pages that don't have a meta description.

3. Finally, click the arrow next to the "Title" column and select "(blank)." This will filter for pages that don't have a title tag.

2. Assessing Your Website's Technical Performance

There are several ways you can assess your website's technical performance. You can either use comprehensive apps that will typically visualize your data for you (such as SEMrush, Ahrefs, or Ubersuggest) or you can use Screaming Frog to export your data and then analyze it in Google Spreadsheets.

To assess your website's technical performance, you'll want to look at

- Your website's speed
- Your website's mobile-friendliness
- Your website's security
- Your website's uptime

If you're using an app, most of this data will be readily available—however, it usually won't give you as much detail as if you were to export the data and analyze it yourself. Very often, such apps give you a "health score" which doesn't always reflect the actual state of your website. Many of the issues they identify may not be actually impacting your website's performance.

If you're using Screaming Frog and Google Spreadsheets, you'll need to do a bit more digging. On the other hand, you'll be able to get a lot more detail and identify issues that most apps may not flag.

Website Speed

For this part, you'll need to connect PageSpeed Insights to Screaming Frog. To assess your website's speed, you'll want to look at the "Time to First Byte,[5]" "Download Time,[6]" and "Redirect Path[7]" columns. If you see

---

[5] Time to First Byte (TTFB) is the amount of time it takes for a web browser to receive the first byte of data from a server after making a request. TTFB is a critical metric for website performance, as it is often used as an indicator of how quickly a website is able to respond to requests and deliver content. A fast TTFB can help to improve the user experience and can indirectly impact a website's search engine ranking, as Google's algorithm considers page speed as an important factor for ranking. TTFB can be influenced by a number of factors, such as server response time, network latency, and content delivery network (CDN) performance.

[6] Download time refers to the amount of time it takes for a web page or file to fully load and be displayed in a web browser. Download time is an important aspect of website performance, as it directly impacts the user experience and can influence user engagement, bounce rates, and conversion rates. A fast download time can help to improve user satisfaction and indirectly impact a website's search engine ranking, as Google's algorithm considers page speed as an important factor for ranking. Download time can be influenced by a number of factors, such as server response time, network latency, file size, and page complexity.

[7] Redirect path refers to the sequence of HTTP requests and server responses that occur when a user or search engine bot tries to access a web page that has been moved or deleted. When a page is moved or deleted, a web server will typically send a redirect response, such as a 301 or 302 redirect, to the user's browser or search engine, indicating the new location of the page. Redirect path can be used to diagnose issues with redirects and to ensure that they are set up correctly, as it shows the sequence of redirects that occur and can help to identify redirect chains or loops.

any pages that have a high "Time to First Byte" or "Download Time," you'll want to investigate further as this could be indicative of a slow website. Additionally, if there are any pages with a long "Redirect Path," you'll also want to investigate as this could be impacting your website's speed.

Here are the benchmarks you should be aiming for:

- Time to First Byte: Should be less than 200ms.

- Download Time: Should be less than 3 seconds.

- Redirect Path: Not more than one—each redirect will add additional time onto your page's load time, causing annoyance to users and lowering your PageSpeed score.

Mobile-Friendliness

To assess your website's mobile-friendliness, you'll want to look at the "Viewport[8]" column. If you see any pages that don't have a viewport specified, this means that the page is not optimized for mobile and should be fixed.

How to Fix It

Adding a viewport is relatively simple—you just need to add the following tag to the head of your page:

---

[8] Viewport is a term used in web design and development to describe the visible area of a web page within a web browser. The size and dimensions of the viewport can vary depending on the device and browser being used and can impact how a web page is displayed and how users interact with it. In responsive web design, viewport is an important consideration, as it is used to determine how a web page should be scaled and laid out to provide an optimal user experience across different devices. By setting the viewport meta tag in the HTML head of a page, web developers can specify how a web page should be displayed on mobile devices.

```
<meta name="viewport" content="width=device-width,
initial-scale=1.0">
```

This will ensure that your page is correctly sized for mobile devices. However, you may also need to make additional changes to optimize your page for mobile—such as increasing the font size or making sure that your buttons are large enough to be clicked easily. To conduct further mobile optimizations, use Google's Mobile-Friendly Test tool to get specific suggestions.

Security

To assess your website's security, you'll want to look at the "SSL[9]" column. If you see any pages that are marked as "Non-secure," this means that the page is not SSL encrypted and is therefore not secure. These pages should be fixed as soon as possible.

How to Fix It

If you want to add SSL to your website, you'll need to purchase an SSL certificate and then install it on your server. This can usually be done through your hosting provider. Once you have installed the SSL certificate, you'll need to update your website's code so that all pages are served over HTTPS instead of HTTP.

---

[9] SSL (Secure Sockets Layer) is a security protocol used to establish a secure and encrypted connection between a web server and a web browser. SSL is used to protect sensitive information, such as passwords, credit card numbers, and personal data, from being intercepted by malicious third parties. When a website is secured with SSL, a padlock icon is displayed in the web browser's address bar, indicating that the connection is secure. SSL has been largely replaced by the newer and more secure TLS (Transport Layer Security) protocol, but the term SSL is still commonly used to refer to encrypted connections in general.

Uptime

To assess your website's uptime, you'll want to look at the "Response Code[10]" column. If you see any pages that have a response code of "5xx," this means that the page is down and is not currently accessible. These pages should be fixed as soon as possible.

How to Fix It

If you see that a page is down, the first thing you should do is check your server to see if it is up and running. If the server is down, you'll need to contact your hosting provider to have them fix the issue. If the server is up and running but the page is still down, this could be caused by an issue with the page's code. In this case, you'll need to contact a developer to have them take a look and fix the issue.

Other Issues

Additionally, you can bulk-check for other common issues such as

- Pages with no meta tags

- Pages with no H1 tags

- Pages with more than one H1 tag

- Pages with long titles

- Pages with short titles

---

[10] Response code refers to the three-digit status codes that are returned by web servers in response to HTTP requests from web browsers or other clients. Response codes are used to provide information about the status of the requested resource and the success or failure of the request. The most common response codes are 2xx, which indicate success; 3xx, which indicate redirection; 4xx, which indicate client errors; and 5xx, which indicate server errors. Response codes can be used to diagnose issues with web pages, such as broken links or server errors, and are an important part of web development and troubleshooting.

- Pages with long meta descriptions

- Pages with short meta descriptions

The easiest way to do this is to export your Screaming Frog data and organize it in one spreadsheet. Then you and your team can easily spot-check for common issues that are relevant to your website and flag them with the key stakeholders.

3. Analyzing Your Interlinking Structure and Link Placement

Once you have Screaming Frog data for your website, you can also use it to analyze your interlinking structure and link placement. This is important because your interlinking structure can impact both your SEO and your website's usability.

To start, you'll want to look at the "Inlinks" column. This will show you all of the pages on your website that are linked to from other pages. You can use this data to assess whether or not your website has a good balance of links. A well-linked website will have a mix of internal links (links to other pages on the same website) and external links (links to other websites).

If you see that a page has a lot of external links and very few internal links, this could be an indication that the page is being used as a link farm. This is bad for both SEO and usability, as it confuses search engines and makes it difficult for users to navigate your website.

To fix this issue, you'll want to add more internal links to the page. You can do this by linking to other relevant pages on your website from within the content of the page. For example, if you have a page about cat toys, you could link to other pages on your website that discuss related topics, such as cat food, cat health, or cat breeds.

You can also use the "Inlinks" data to assess the placement of your links. Ideally, your links should be placed within the body of your content, rather than in the sidebar or footer. This is because links placed within the body of content are more likely to be clicked by users, which can help to improve your website's usability.

To fix this issue, you'll want to move any links that are in the sidebar or footer into the body of your content. You can do this by editing the code of your website. If you're not comfortable doing this yourself, you'll need to hire a developer to do it for you.

4. Identifying Content to Update, Rewrite, or Remove

Once you have Screaming Frog data for your website, you can also use it to identify content that needs to be updated, rewritten, or removed. This is important because outdated or irrelevant content can hurt both your SEO and your website's usability.

To start, you'll want to look at the "Content" column. This will show you all of the content on your website, as well as the date that it was last updated. You can use this data to assess which pieces of content are outdated and need to be updated.

If you see that a piece of content is more than two years old, this is generally an indication that it is outdated and needs to be updated. Of course, there are some exceptions to this rule. For example, if you have a piece of content that is about a timeless topic, such as the history of your company, then it may not need to be updated as frequently.

To update outdated content, you'll want to add new information to it and/or change the date that it was last updated. For example, if you have a blog post that is two years old, you could add new information to it, such as updated statistics, reports, or new insights.

In addition to looking for outdated content, you'll also want to look for content that is irrelevant or no longer relevant to your website. This can happen for a number of reasons, such as if your website has changed its focus, if a product has been discontinued, or if an event is no longer happening.

If you find content that is no longer relevant to your website, you'll want to either remove it or update it so that it is relevant again. For example, if you have a blog post about a product that has been discontinued, you could update the post to discuss a similar product that is still available.

The most common method of assessing which pieces of content you should rewrite or update is looking at the data from Google Analytics:

- The content needs removing or rewriting if the average time on page is less than 30 seconds.

- The content needs updating if the number of pageviews is declining.

- The content needs rewriting if the bounce rate is high.

You can find those numbers in Google Analytics by going to Behavior ➤ Site Content ➤ All Pages. To automate this part of the audit, export the data from Google Analytics and analyze it in Google Spreadsheets.

5. Analyzing the Keywords You Already Rank for, Their Relevancy, and Conversion Potential

The next step in conducting a content audit is to analyze the keywords that you already rank for, as well as their relevancy and conversion potential. You can do this by exporting data from Google Search Console and opening it in Google Spreadsheets.

Once you have the data exported, you'll want to look at the following columns:

- Impressions: This column shows you how many people have seen your website in the search results.

- CTR: This column stands for "click-through rate" and shows you what percentage of people who saw your website in the search results clicked it.

- Position: This column shows you what position your website ranks in for a particular keyword.

- Queries: This column shows you the keywords that you rank for.

You can use this data to assess which keywords are most relevant to your website and have the potential to drive traffic and conversions. For example:

1. If you see a keyword that has a high number of impressions but a low CTR, this could be an indication that the meta title or description is not relevant to your target audience.

2. If you see a keyword with a high CTR and a high position, this could be an indication that the keyword is relevant to your target audience and has the potential to drive traffic and conversions.

3. If you see a keyword with a low CTR and a low position, this could be an indication that the keyword is not relevant to your target audience or that there is strong competition for that keyword.

How to conduct this audit:

1. Export data from Google Search Console and open it in Google Spreadsheets. Then, create the following columns in a new sheet:

    -   Keyword

    -   Relevancy

    -   Conversion Potential

    These are the three factors you will be assessing for each keyword.

2. Begin going through each keyword one by one, and assign a relevancy score from 1 to 5 for each keyword (1 being not relevant at all, 5 being extremely relevant). You can use the following criteria to help you assess relevancy:

    -   Is the keyword related to your product or service?

    -   Do you have a page on your website that is optimized for that keyword?

    -   Is the keyword being searched for by your target audience?

    -   Is the keyword relevant to your business goals?

3. Once you have assessed the relevancy of each keyword, begin assigning a conversion potential score from 1 to 5 for each keyword (1 being low

conversion potential, 5 being high conversion potential). You can use the following criteria to help you assess conversion potential:

- Does the keyword indicate that the searcher is further along in the buying cycle? For example, "buy XYZ product" indicates a higher level of intent than "XYZ product reviews."

- Can you track conversions for this keyword? If not, it will be difficult to know whether or not the keyword has high conversion potential.

4. To make things easier to read, you can highlight cells in each row according to their relevancy score (1–5) or conversion potential score (1–5) using conditional formatting. Simply select the cells you want to format, go to Format ➤ Conditional formatting... ➤ Format cells if..., choose which condition you want to apply, select Custom formula is, type in =$B2>=4 (or whatever number/condition you want), then click Done twice. Select your desired formatting options. Click Done once again.

5. After you have assessed the relevancy and conversion potential of each keyword, you can begin to prioritize which keywords you want to focus on. For example, you may want to focus on keywords with high relevancy and high conversion potential. Or, you may want to focus on keywords with high relevancy and low competition. The decision is up to you, depending on your business goals and needs. Typically, businesses with a smaller organic footprint would start from optimizing for

keywords with the lowest competition and high search volume to increase brand awareness. If you already get a decent amount of organic traffic, but lack conversions, you may want to focus on those keywords with high conversion potential first.

6. Calculating Your Current and Future ROI

Current ROI from Organic Search

There are two primary ways to measure the ROI from organic search, conversion rate and revenue per visit:

- **Conversion rate** is the percentage of visitors who take a desired action (e.g., make a purchase, sign up for a newsletter, etc.).

- **Revenue per visit** is the total revenue generated by visitors divided by the number of visits.

You can calculate your current organic search conversion rate and revenue per visit with the following formulas:

- Conversion rate = (# of conversions / # of visits) × 100

- Revenue per visit = (total revenue / # of visits)

Once you have these numbers, you can calculate your current ROI from organic search using this formula:

$$ROI = ((\text{revenue per visit} \times \text{conversion rate}) - \text{cost per click}) / \text{cost per click}) \times 100$$

For example, let's say you have a website that generates $100,000 in revenue from 10,000 visitors per month. Of those 10,000 visitors, 2% convert into paying customers. You're currently spending $5000 per month on PPC advertising to generate these results. In this scenario, your current ROI from organic search would be

$$(((\$100,000 \,/\, 10,000) \times 2\%) - \$5000) \,/\, \$5000) \times 100 = 200\%$$

Forecasting Future ROI with Potential SEO Optimizations

Now that you know how to calculate your current ROI from organic search, you can use that information to forecast the potential ROI of various SEO optimizations. To do this effectively, you need to identify which keywords are currently driving traffic and conversions on your website and which keywords have potential to drive even more traffic and conversions with some optimization.

Once you've identified these keywords, you can use industry benchmarks to estimate the potential impact of optimizations on traffic and conversions for each keyword. For example, if you're currently ranking in position #5 for a certain keyword with 5% conversion rate and 1000 monthly searches, optimizing for position #1 could increase your traffic from 50 to 400 sessions per month while also increasing click-through rate (CTR) by eight times.[11]

Using these benchmarks along with your current traffic and conversion data points, you can come up with estimates for the potential increase in traffic and conversions that various optimizations could provide for

---

[11] Bailyn, E. (2022). "Google Click-Through Rates (CTRs) by Ranking Position in 2023." [online] First Page Sage. Available at https://firstpagesage.com/seo-blog/google-click-through-rates-ctrs-by-ranking-position/ [Accessed Feb. 19, 2023].

different keywords. From there, it's simply a matter of using the same ROI formula as before to measure the potential return on investment for each optimization opportunity.

For example, let's say you've identified a keyword that you're currently ranking in position 5 for with 500 monthly searches and a 2% conversion rate. Based on industry benchmarks, you believe that optimizing for position 1 could increase traffic by 50% and increase conversion rate by three times. Using these assumptions, you can estimate that optimizing for this keyword could result in the following increase in monthly traffic and conversions:

Monthly traffic: $500 \times 1.5 = 750$

Monthly conversions: $500 \times 0.02 \times 3 = 30$

With this increase in traffic and conversions, you can estimate that your ROI from organic search would increase by 150%:

$(((\$100,000 / 750) \times 30\%) - \$5000) / \$5000) \times 100 = 150\%$

As you can see, even a small optimization like this can have a big impact on your ROI from organic search. And as you continue to optimize your website and improve your rankings for more and more keywords, the ROI from organic search will continue to increase.

7. Auditing Your Website's Backlink Profile for Quality and Relevance

The quality of your website's backlink profile is one of the most important ranking factors in Google's algorithm. In general, the more high-quality, relevant backlinks you have pointing to your website, the higher your website will rank in search results.

To see what kind of backlinks you currently have pointing to your website, you can use Google Search Console. Simply go to the "Links to Your Site" section and you'll see a list of all the websites that are linking to yours, as well as the number of links each website is sending.

Now, you don't want just any website linking to yours. You want high-quality websites in your niche that are likely to send targeted traffic to your website. So, how do you determine the quality of a website's backlink profile?

There are a few different metrics you can look at, but the two most important ones are Domain Authority (DA) and PageRank:

- **Domain Authority** is a metric created by Moz that predicts how well a website will rank in search engine results pages (SERPs). It's based on a number of factors, including the age of the domain, the number of inbound links, and the quality of those inbound links.

- **PageRank** is a metric created by Google that also predicts how well a website will rank in SERPs. It's based on the number of inbound links pointing to a website, as well as the quality of those inbound links.

In general, you want websites with high DA and PageRank linking to yours. You can check DA and PageRank for any website using Moz's free Open Site Explorer tool. Simply enter the URL of the website into the tool, and it will show you the DA and PageRank for that site.

Now that you know how to check the quality of a website's backlink profile, you can start auditing your own. Export the list of websites linking to yours in Google Search Console and open it with Google Spreadsheets. Next, sort the domains by the number of links they're sending to your website (high to low). Then, use Moz's Open Site Explorer tool to check the DA and PageRank for each domain and input those numbers in new columns.

As you're auditing your backlink profile, keep an eye out for any low-quality or irrelevant websites linking to yours. If you find any, reach out to the webmaster and ask them to remove the link. This will help improve the quality of your backlink profile and, as a result, your search engine rankings.

If you can't get a website to remove a low-quality or irrelevant link pointing to your website, you can "disavow" it. This essentially tells Google to ignore that link when determining your website's search engine rankings.

To disavow a link, create a text file with the list of all the low-quality or irrelevant domains linking to your website. Then, go to search.google.com/search-console/disavow-links and upload that file to Google Search Console.

Setting Benchmarks and Goals for Your Website's SXO Performance

Now that you have analyzed your website's current search experience, it's time to set some benchmarks and goals. This will help you track your progress and ensure that your SXO efforts are paying off.

There are a few different metrics you can use to benchmark and measure your website's SXO performance, including

- Search engine rankings

- Organic traffic

- Conversion rate

- Revenue

Step 1: Prepare a Document to Track Your Progress

To get started, create a new document in Google Spreadsheets and input your website's current performance levels for each of the preceding metrics. Then, create new columns for where you want your website to be in three months, six months, and one year.

Step 2: Know Your Target Audience

Understanding your target audience is essential for setting SXO goals that will actually resonate with them. For example, if your target audience is 18–24-year-olds, you're not going to want to set a goal to improve your website's search engine rankings for the term "retirement planning."

Questions to answer:

- Who is your target audience?

- What are their needs?

- What are their interests?

- What type of language do they use?

- Where do they live?

- What is their age range?

- What is their gender?

Step 3: Identify Your Products or Services

The next step is to identify your products or services. What do you offer that your target audience needs or wants?

Understanding your products or services is essential for setting SXO goals that will actually help you sell more. For example, if you're selling cat toys, you're not going to want to set a goal to improve your website's search engine rankings for the term "dog food."

Questions to answer:

- What products or services do you offer?
- Who is your target audience for each product or service?
- What needs does each product or service meet?
- What are the key features of each product or service?
- How are your products or services different from your competitors?

Step 4: Set Realistic Goals

Now that you know your target audience and what you're selling, it's time to set some realistic SXO goals. These should be specific, measurable, achievable, relevant, and time-bound (SMART).

Some examples of SMART SXO goals include

- Increase organic traffic by 10% in the next three months
- Improve conversion rates by 2% in the next six months
- Increase revenue by 50% in the next year
- Get 1000 new email subscribers in the next year

Step 5: Decide Which Tools You Will Use

There are a variety of different tools you can use to help you achieve your SXO goals. These include things like keyword research tools, analytics tools, and conversion rate optimization tools.

The best way to decide which tools you need is to take a look at your goals and then determine which tools will help you achieve those goals.

For example, if your goal is to increase organic traffic, you might want to invest in an advanced keyword research tool to help you find new keywords to target.

Step 6: Create a Timeline

Once you have your goals and tools set, it's time to create a timeline. This will help you stay on track and make sure you're making progress toward your goals.

A timeline for SXO might look something like this:

- Month 1: Research target audience and set goals

- Month 2: Conduct keyword research and begin optimizing website structure

- Month 3: Create compelling content and improve website design

- Month 4: Test and measure results, experiment, and iterate

Following a timeline like this will help you slowly but surely make progress toward your SXO goals.

Key Takeaways

Improving your website's SXO performance is a multistep process that involves analyzing your website's search experience, gathering data with various tools, and setting benchmarks and goals. By following these steps, you can gain a better understanding of your website's users, optimize your website for search engines, and ultimately drive more traffic and revenue to your business.

Some key takeaways from this section include

- Understanding your website's current search experience is the first step in applying SXO (search experience optimization) to your website. This includes looking at search engine visibility, keyword targeting, website structure, content, design, and conversions.

- There are several tools available to conduct a search experience audit, including Google Analytics, Google Search Console, Screaming Frog, Microsoft Clarity, Google Spreadsheets, Google Looker Studio, Google PageSpeed Insights, and Google Tag Manager.

- Setting benchmarks and goals for your website's SXO performance is important to track progress and ensure that your efforts are paying off.

- Metrics such as search engine rankings, organic traffic, conversion rate, and revenue can be used to benchmark and measure your website's SXO performance.

- Set realistic, SMART SXO goals such as increasing organic traffic, improving conversion rates, and increasing revenue.

- Determine which tools you need based on your goals, such as keyword research tools, analytics tools, and conversion rate optimization tools.

- Create a timeline to stay on track and make progress toward your SXO goals, including research, keyword optimization, content creation, and testing and measuring results.

Identifying Your Target Audience

When determining your target audience, a good place to start is by considering your current customer base. Who are the people that are already buying your products or using your services? What do they have in common? Are there any demographic trends that you can identify? For example, if you sell women's cosmetics, your target audience is likely to be female. Once you have a basic understanding of who your current customers are, you can begin to define your ideal customer.

Gathering Customer Insights

One of the best places to start when trying to identify your target audience is to take a look at your current customer base. Who are the people that are already buying your products or services?

Why Are Customer Insights Important?

In order to deliver an amazing search experience that converts, you need to understand your customers. This understanding comes from knowing their needs, wants, desires, frustrations, and how they make decisions. Customer insights allow you to generate targeted content, improve the user experience on your website, and fix any potential conversion roadblocks. In short, if you want your SXO strategy to be successful, you need to start with customer insights. Luckily, there are a variety of ways to gather those insights:

- Feedback questionnaires: You can reach out to your customers directly by sending feedback questionnaires. These can be simple surveys that ask customers about their recent experience with your website or product. You can also use questionnaires to gauge customer satisfaction or get suggestions for improvements. Feedback questionnaires are an easy way to get direct input from your customers that can be used to improve the search experience on your website.

- Reviews: Online reviews are another great way to get insight into what your customers think about your website or product. Reading through reviews can help you identify any areas where customers are struggling as well as any areas where you're excelling. Use this information to improve the search experience on your website and increase conversion rates.

- Customer sentiment surveys: Customer sentiment surveys provide valuable insights into how customers feel about your brand or product. These surveys can be used to understand both positive and negative sentiment around your brand. This information can then be used to improve the search experience on your website and make sure that visitors have a positive experience when they interact with your brand online.

- Behavioral data: Another method of gathering customer insights is through behavioral data analysis. This type of analysis looks at how users interact with your website, what pages they visit, how long they stay on each page, and what actions they take while using your site. This data can be extremely useful in understanding the customer journey and identifying any areas where users might be getting stuck during their interactions with your site. By understanding behavioral data, you can make changes to improve the search experience on your website and increase conversion rates.

- A/B testing: A/B testing is a great way to test different versions of your website or product and see which one performs better with users. This type of testing allows you to iterate on your design in a way that is informed by data rather than guesswork. By conducting A/B tests on different elements of your website or product, you can gather valuable insights into what works best for users.

- Social listening: Social media provides a wealth of information about what people think about your brand or product. You can use social media platforms like Twitter and Facebook to listen for mentions of your company. This will give you valuable insights into how people perceive you. You can also use social media monitoring tools like Hootsuite to track mentions of your brand across the Internet.

- Support tickets: Reviewing support tickets is another great way to get insight into what customers think about your brand or product. This type of feedback provides valuable information about areas where customers are struggling as well as compliments that you can use in your marketing materials. By reviewing support tickets, you can gain valuable insight into your customers' needs.

- Chatbot data: If you have a chatbot on your website, then you have access to valuable data that can be used to understand your customers' needs. Chatbot data includes information like the questions people are asking, what topics they are interested in, and what problems they are trying to solve. This information can then be used to improve the content on your website, making it more relevant and useful for your target audience.

Now that you know the different ways to gather customer insights, it's time to use this information to define your ideal customer. This can be done by creating customer persona.

Defining Your Ideal Customer

Once you have a better understanding of your current customer base, you can start to define your ideal customer (persona). This is the person that you want to target with your SXO efforts.

When defining your ideal customer, you should consider things like

1. **Demographics**

   One of the first things that you should consider when trying to identify your target audience is demographics. This includes

   - Age

   - Gender

   - Location

   - Marital status

   - Number of children

- Employment status

- Income level

- Education level

Knowing the demographics of your target audience will help you to understand what their needs and wants are. It will also help you to identify the best channels to reach them.

2. **Psychographics**

   Psychographics refer to the psychological characteristics of your ideal customer. This includes things like

   - Personality type

   - Values

   - Interests

   - Lifestyle

   - Behaviors

   Psychographics can be extremely helpful in determining what motivates your target audience and how to best reach them.

3. **Needs**

   Another important factor to consider when trying to identify your target audience is needs. This includes

   - What problem are they trying to solve?

   - What need do they have that is not being met?

   - What are their goals?

When you understand the needs of your target audience, you can create content that addresses those needs and helps them to solve their problem.

4. **Challenges and pain points**

   In addition to needs, you should also consider the challenges and pain points of your target audience. This includes

   - What are their biggest frustrations?

   - What are their frustrations?

   - What are the obstacles they face?

   - What makes their life difficult?

   Addressing these challenges and pain points in your marketing will help you to better connect with your target audience. Include both general challenges as well as specific challenges that are relevant to your product or service.

5. **Goals**

   It's also important to consider the goals of your target audience. This includes

   - What are they trying to achieve?

   - What are their long-term goals?

   - What are their short-term goals?

Understanding the goals of your target customer will help you to create products or services that they need and want.

Defining your target audience is an important step in the SXO process. By taking the time to understand who your ideal customer is, you will be able to create a more targeted and effective SXO strategy.

Now that you know the different factors to consider when trying to identify your target audience, it's time to start creating your customer persona.

Create Your Customer Persona

Creating a customer persona is a great way to help you focus your SXO efforts. When done correctly, it will help you to better understand your target audience and create content that is relevant to their needs.

There are a few different methods that you can use to create your customer persona:

1. **The five Ws**

   One of the simplest methods is to use the five Ws. In this method, you answer the following questions:

   - Who: Who is your target audience?

   - What: What are their needs?

   - When: When do they need your product or service?

   - Where: Where do they live?

   - Why: Why do they need your product or service?

   Answering these questions will help you to create a basic customer persona.

2. **The four Cs**

   Another popular method for creating a customer persona is the four Cs. This method focuses on the following factors:

   - Context: What is the current situation of your target audience?

- Challenges: What are the challenges and pain points of your target audience?

- Considerations: What are the goals of your target audience?

- Changes: What factors influence the decision-making process of your target audience?

3. **Custom templates**

   If you want to get a little more detailed with your customer persona, you can use a custom template. There are a number of different templates available online, or you can create your own by following these steps:

   1) **Develop a profile**

      Once you have identified the needs and wants of your target audience, the next step is to develop a profile for your customer persona. This profile should include information such as name, age, gender, occupation, interests, and so on. The goal here is to create a fictional character that represents your ideal customer.

   2) **Give them a face**

      One way to make your customer persona more relatable is to give them a face. This can be done by finding or creating an image that represents your persona. For example, if your persona is a middle-aged woman, you might find or create an image of a woman in her 40s or 50s.

3) **Create a backstory**

Another way to make your customer persona more relatable is to create a backstory for them. This can include information such as where they grew up, their family life, their education, their work history, and so on. The goal here is to make your persona feel like a real person with a rich history.

4) **Make them real**

Once you have created a profile, given them a face, and created a backstory, the next step is to make your persona feel real. This can be done by giving them a voice. For example, you might create a short bio for your persona that includes their name, age, occupation, and interests. You can also create a list of quotes that your persona might say.

Use Google Analytics to Learn More About Your Audience

Google Analytics is a powerful tool that can be used to learn more about your target audience. By understanding the demographics, interests, and behavior of your website visitors, you will be able to create a more targeted SXO strategy.

There are a few different ways that you can use Google Analytics to learn more about your target audience:

1. Demographics

   One of the first things that you can do is check the demographics of your website visitors. This information can be found in the "Audience" section of Google Analytics. Here, you will be able to see the age, gender, and location of your website visitors.

2. Interests

   Another thing that you can do is check the interests of your website visitors. This information can be found in the "Audience" section of Google Analytics. Here, you will be able to see the affinity categories,[12] in-market segments,[13] and other interests of your website visitors.

---

[12] Affinity categories are a type of audience segment in Google Ads that are based on users' long-term interests and habits. Affinity categories are generated by analyzing data from users' web browsing activity, search history, and other online behavior and are used to target ads to users who have shown an interest in certain topics or categories. There are a variety of affinity categories available in Google Ads, such as "Food and Dining," "Sports and Fitness," and "Travel." By targeting ads to users in specific affinity categories, advertisers can reach audiences who are more likely to be interested in their products or services.

[13] In-market segments are a type of audience segment in Google Ads that are based on users' recent search and browsing behavior and indicate a current interest or intent to purchase a particular product or service. In-market segments are generated by analyzing data from users' web browsing activity and search history and are used to target ads to users who are actively researching or considering a purchase. There are a variety of in-market segments available in Google Ads, such as "Travel," "Real Estate," and "Automotive." By targeting ads to users in specific in-market segments, advertisers can reach audiences who are more likely to be ready to make a purchase.

3. Behavior

Another thing that you can do is check the behavior
of your website visitors. This information can be
found in the "Behavior" section of Google Analytics.
Here, you will be able to see how often people visit
your website, what pages they visit, how long they
stay on each page, and so on.

Additionally, you can use Google Analytics to segment your traffic. This
can help you to see which keywords and traffic sources are bringing in the
most valuable customers.

To segment your traffic in Google Analytics:

1. Log in to your Google Analytics account.

2. Click the "Admin" tab in the left navigation panel.

3. In the "Property" column, click "All Traffic Sources."

4. Click the "Segment" drop-down menu and select
    "New Segment."

5. Name your segment and select the traffic source (e.g., direct,[14] referral,[15] social,[16] paid search[17]) that you want to include in the segment.

6. Click the "Condition" drop-down menu and select the condition (e.g., equals, contains, starts with) that you want to apply to the segment.

7. Enter the value for the condition (e.g., direct).

8. Click the "Create Segment" button.

---

[14] Direct traffic refers to visits to a website that occur when a user types the URL of the website directly into their web browser or clicks on a bookmark or link that they have saved. Direct traffic is an important source of website traffic, as it represents users who are already familiar with the website and are likely to be loyal customers or fans. Direct traffic can be influenced by a number of factors, such as brand recognition, offline advertising, and word-of-mouth referrals.

[15] Referral traffic refers to visits to a website that occur when a user clicks a link to the website from another website or social media platform. Referral traffic is an important source of website traffic, as it can represent users who are interested in the website's content and are likely to engage with it. Referral traffic can be influenced by a number of factors, such as backlinks, social media sharing, and online advertising.

[16] Social traffic refers to visits to a website that occur when a user clicks a link to the website from a social media platform, such as Facebook, Twitter, or LinkedIn. Social traffic is an important source of website traffic, as it can represent users who are interested in the website's content and are likely to engage with it. Social traffic can be influenced by a number of factors, such as social media marketing, sharing and commenting on social media, and social media advertising.

[17] Paid search traffic refers to visits to a website that occur as a result of paid advertising on search engines, such as Google Ads or Bing Ads. Paid search traffic is an important source of website traffic for businesses that want to attract new customers, as it allows them to target specific keywords and audiences with their ads. Paid search traffic can be influenced by a number of factors, such as keyword selection, ad quality and relevance, and bid strategy.

9. You will now see the segmented data in your Google Analytics account.

10. Repeat steps 5–9 for each traffic source that you want to include in the segmentation.

By understanding the demographics, interests, and behavior of your website visitors, you will be able to create a more targeted SXO strategy.

Key Takeaways

The success of any digital marketing strategy relies on understanding your target audience. Now you know how to identify and define your ideal customer, which is a crucial step in developing a targeted SXO strategy. By gathering customer insights through methods like feedback questionnaires, reviews, and social listening, you can better understand your customers' needs, wants, frustrations, and decision-making processes.

Some key takeaways from this section include

- Identifying your target audience is an important step in creating an effective search experience optimization (SXO) strategy.

- To identify your target audience, start by gathering customer insights and analyzing demographic and psychographic factors, as well as their needs, challenges, pain points, and goals.

- Use customer insights gathered from various sources such as feedback questionnaires, reviews, customer sentiment surveys, behavioral data analysis, A/B testing, social listening, support tickets, and chatbot data.

- Define your ideal customer by creating a customer persona, which can be done using various methods such as the five Ws, the four Cs, or custom templates.

- Google Analytics is a powerful tool that can be used to learn more about your target audience and create a more targeted SXO strategy by analyzing demographics, interests, behavior, and traffic sources.

Keyword Research

After you have identified your target audience, the next step is to do some keyword research in order to find new content opportunities. There are a number of different tools and methods that you can use for keyword research, but the most important thing is to make sure that you are targeting keywords that your target audience is actually searching for.

Brainstorming

One of the most effective methods of keyword research is brainstorming with other teams and stakeholders at your company. By getting input from a variety of sources, you can come up with a comprehensive list of potential keywords that you might not have thought of on your own. Other teams can often have valuable insights into the language used by your target audience.

The first step in this approach is to identify which teams would be most helpful in the keyword brainstorming process. For example, if you're optimizing a website for a hotel, it would make sense to involve the sales, marketing, and customer service teams. Once you've identified the relevant teams, the next step is to schedule a meeting (or series of meetings) and come up with a plan for how you'll approach the task.

Examples of teams that might be helpful in keyword brainstorming:

1. **Sales**

   Your sales team is on the front lines of your business, dealing directly with customers and prospects on a daily basis. They have a wealth of knowledge about what people are searching for and what kind of language they use when they're looking for products or services like yours. Because of this, they can be a valuable resource when it comes to brainstorming new keywords for your SXO efforts.

   Ask them to share any insights they have about what people are searching for and what terminology they use. It's also helpful to ask if there are any pain points that prospects frequently bring up or if there are any areas where your competitors seem to be outperforming you.

2. **Customer service**

   Much like your sales team, your customer service reps deal directly with customers on a daily basis. They field calls and answer questions all day long, so they likely have a good idea of the kinds of things people are searching for when they call in. Additionally, because they're often the first point of contact for many customers, they may also be able to provide insights into common pain points or areas where your company could improve.

Ask them to share any insights they have about customer searches or common issues that arise. Also, find out if there are any areas where you could provide more information or if there are any topics that customers frequently call about.

3. **Marketing**

    Your marketing team is responsible for generating awareness and interest in your company's products or services. As such, they likely have a good understanding of the kinds of keywords that convert into customers. They can also provide insights into how your target audience thinks about your industry and what language they use when they're searching for information.

    Ask them to share any insights they have about their messaging and its effectiveness. Additionally, find out more about each channel and what kinds of terms, hashtags, or emojis perform best on each platform. Finally, ask if there are any new initiatives or campaigns that might be relevant to your SXO efforts.

4. **IT/technical**

    If you're optimizing a website for a technical product or service, it's important to involve your IT or technical team in the brainstorming process. They likely have a good understanding of the language used by people in your industry and can provide valuable insights into the types of things people are searching for.

Ask them to share any insights they have about the technical aspects of your product or service. Additionally, find out if there are any common issues that people run into or if there are any areas where you could provide more information.

There are a few different ways you could use to brainstorm keywords with other teams:

1. Mind mapping: This involves creating a central concept or topic and then branches off of that concept with related ideas. For example, if you're mind mapping keywords for a hotel website, you might start with "hotel" in the center and then branch off to "room," "restaurant," "gym," "spa," etc.

2. Questions: You can simply ask people from other teams questions about the kinds of searches they see and what vocabulary is used. For example, you might ask a customer service rep, "What are the most common questions people have about our product?" or ask a salesperson, "What are some of the words prospects use when inquiring about our product?"

3. Word association: This technique involves saying a word out loud and then having someone else say the first word that comes to mind in response. For example, if you start with the word "car," the next person might say "driving," "road," etc. You can keep going until you run out of ideas. This technique can be especially helpful in getting creative with new keyword ideas.

Trending Keyword Research

The next step is to research the trending keywords in your industry. This will give you an idea of the kinds of terms people are searching for right now and what topics are popular.

There are a few different ways to research trending keywords:

1. Google Trends: This is a free tool from Google that lets you see how often particular terms are being searched for.

2. Social media: Check out popular hashtags on social media platforms like Twitter, Instagram, and Facebook.

3. News sites: Have a look at what's trending on popular news sites like BBC, CNN, and Fox News.

4. Industry-specific sites: Have a look at what's trending on popular sites in your industry. For example, if you're in the tech industry, you could check out Mashable, TechCrunch, or The Next Web.

In this book, we'll focus on using Google Trends to research trending keywords.

Step 1: Enter a Seed Keyword into Google Trends

The first step is to enter a seed keyword into Google Trends. A seed keyword is a broad term that describes the topic that you want to write about. For example, if we want to write about SEO, our seed keyword could be "SEO."

If you're not sure which seed keyword to use, try brainstorming a list of potential topics that you could write about. Once you have a list of potential topics, you can use Google Trends to see which ones are being searched for the most.

To use Google Trends, simply go to *trends.google.com/trends/*. Then, enter your seed keyword into the "Search" bar and click "Enter."

Step 2: Narrow Down Your Results by Location and Timeframe

Once you've entered your seed keyword and hit "Enter," you'll be taken to a page with results for that keyword. By default, Google Trends will show results for the past 12 months in all locations. However, you can narrow down your results by location and timeframe using the "Location" and "Time" filters at the top of the page.

For example, if we wanted to see results for our "SEO" seed keyword in the United States for the past year, we would select "United States" from the "Location" drop-down menu and "Past 12 months" from the "Time" drop-down menu. Then, we would click "Apply."

You can also select multiple locations or timeframes by clicking them while holding down the Ctrl key (Windows) or Command key (Mac).

Step 3: Analyze Your Results

Once you've narrowed down your results by location and timeframe, it's time to analyze your results. There are a few different ways that you can do this.

Use the "Interest over time" graph to see how interest in your keyword has changed over time. The blue line represents searches for your keyword, while the red line represents searches for all other keywords.

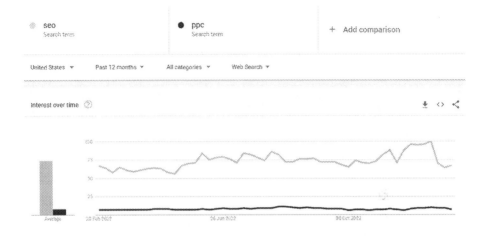

Look at the related topics section to see what other topics are related to your keyword. You can use this section to generate ideas for new blog posts or articles.

Evergreen Keyword Research

An evergreen keyword is a keyword that is relevant all year round and does not go out of style. Evergreen keywords are an important part of any SEO or content marketing strategy because they can be used to generate traffic and leads throughout the year. If you can identify and target evergreen keywords, you'll be able to sustainably grow your traffic and leads over time.

For example, "SEO" is an evergreen keyword because it is always relevant to people who are interested in marketing and online visibility. On the other hand, "Christmas tree" is not an evergreen keyword because it is only relevant during the Christmas season.

To find evergreen keywords, the best place to start is with Google's Keyword Planner tool. This tool is designed for people who want to run advertising campaigns on Google, but it can also be used for keyword research.

To use the Keyword Planner tool, go to ads.google.com/intl/en_us/ home/. Next, log in or create your Google Ads account. Then, click the "Tools" tab and select "Keyword Planner."

Next, click "Discover new keywords" and enter a seed keyword into the "Enter products or services closely related to your business" field. Then, click "Get results."

On the next page, you'll see a list of related keywords. You can use the "Avg. monthly searches" column to see how many people are searching for each keyword per month. In the top-right corner, you can also switch between a list of keywords and groups to browse entire clusters of related queries.

To find evergreen keywords, you'll want to focus on keywords with high search volume throughout the year. You can use the "Seasonality" filter to see which keywords are being searched for the most during different times of the year. However, keep in mind that not all relevant keywords with high search volume will be a good fit for your strategy. You'll also want to make sure that the keywords you choose are relevant to have low competition. How can you determine this? Look at the number of ads that are being run for each keyword. The more competitive a keyword is, the more ads there will be.

Another factor to consider is the CPC (cost per click). This is the amount that you would need to pay for each click on your ad if you were to run an advertising campaign for that keyword. The CPC can give you an idea of how competitive a keyword is. To view the CPC for each keyword, click the "Keyword ideas" tab and scroll down to the "Avg. CPC" column.

Competitor Keyword Research

Step 1: Identify Your Competitors

The first step in researching your competitors' keyword strategies is to identify who your competitors are. Depending on your industry and niche, you may have different types of competitors. For example, if you are a small business owner selling handcrafted jewelry, your main competitors may be other small businesses that sell handmade jewelry online. However, if you are a large corporation selling mass-produced jewelry, your main competitors may be other large corporations that sell mass-produced jewelry in brick-and-mortar stores. Once you have identified your main competitors, you can begin researching their keyword strategies.

To find out what keywords your competitors are targeting, you can use a variety of free tools available on the Web, such as Google Ads Keyword Planner and KWFinder. Simply enter your competitors' URL into these tools, and they will generate a list of keywords that are associated with their website. You can also use Google's search results to get an idea of which keywords your competitors are targeting. Simply enter your competitors' URL into Google and take note of the keywords that are listed in the title tags and meta descriptions of their website. Alternatively, use Screaming Frog SEO Spider to crawl your competitors' website and export their metadata in bulk.

Once you have a list of your competitors' keywords, you can begin analyzing their keyword strategies. Look at the keywords they are targeting and try to identify any patterns or common themes. For example, if you notice that most of their keywords are related to a certain product or service, it's likely that they are targeting those keywords in an effort to rank for that particular product or service.

Step 2: Analyze Their Rankings

Once you have compiled a list of keywords that your competitors are targeting, the next step is to analyze their rankings for those keywords. There are a number of free tools available that allow you to do this, such as Moz Keyword Explorer (moz.com/explorer). To use these tools, simply enter the URL of your competitors' website and the keyword that you want to check their ranking for. The tool will then give you their current ranking as well as some other useful data points, such as estimated organic traffic and search volume.

You can also use Google's search results to manually check your competitors' rankings for certain keywords. To do this, simply enter the keyword that you want to check into Google and scroll through the search results until you find your competitors' website. Take note of what position they are in for that particular keyword. If they are not in the top ten results, you may want to consider targeting that keyword yourself as it could be an opportunity for you to rank higher than them.

Step 3: Analyze Their Search Traffic

Another way to research your competitors' keyword strategies is to analyze their search traffic. This can give you insight into which keywords they are getting the most organic traffic from and how they are ranking for those keywords.

There are a number of free tools that you can use to do this, such as Ahref Webmaster Tools available at ahrefs.com/en/webmaster-tools. Simply enter your competitors' URL into these tools, and they will give you an estimate of their organic traffic as well as the keywords that they are getting the most traffic from.

People Also Ask

People Also Ask (PAA) keywords are a type of long-tail keyword that is used to trigger featured snippets in Google searches. Featured snippets are brief answers to searcher queries that appear at the top of the Google search results page. They are designed to give users quick and easy access to the information they are looking for. PAA keywords are an important part of SXO because they can help you improve your search ranking, convert more visitors, and generate more revenue.

How to Research People Also Ask Keywords?

There are a few different methods you can use to research PAA keywords. The first method is to use Google's "People Also Ask" boxes. These boxes appear on the right-hand side of the Google search results page and contain a list of related questions that people have also asked about the topic you searched for. To research PAA keywords using this method, simply enter your target keyword into the Google search bar

113

and scroll down to the "People Also Ask" box. From there, you can click each question to see a list of related questions. You can also use tools like AnswerThePublic and Ahrefs' "Questions" report to research PAA keywords.

AnswerThePublic is a free online tool that generates a list of questions based on a given keyword. To use this tool, simply enter your target keyword into the search bar and select your location (United States, UK, Canada, etc.). Then, click the "Get Questions" button, and you will be presented with a list of questions related to your target keyword. You can then export this data into a CSV file for further analysis. Ahrefs' "Questions" report is a paid tool that allows you to see all the questions that people have asked about a given topic, including both PAA keywords and regular keywords. To use this tool, simply enter your target keyword into the Ahrefs site explorer and click the "Questions" tab in the sidebar menu. From there, you will be presented with a list of questions related to your target keyword. You can then export this data into a CSV file for further analysis.

Evaluating and Organizing Your Keyword Ideas

Once you have a list of potential keywords, it's time to start evaluating and organizing them. There are a few different factors you should take into account when doing this:

- Relevance: How relevant is the keyword to your business or website?

- Search volume: How many people are searching for the keyword?

- Competition: How difficult is it to rank for the keyword?

- Click-through rate: What is the expected click-through rate for the keyword?

You can use a variety of tools to help you with this process. If you're on a budget, you can use the Google Keyword Planner tool as described in the previous section. This tool is free to use and will give you an estimate of the search volume, competition, and click-through rate for a given keyword. If you're willing to spend a bit more money, you can use a paid tool like Ahrefs or SEMrush.

Once you've gathered the data on each keyword, it's time to start organizing them. One way to do this is to create a spreadsheet with the following columns:

- Keyword

- Search volume

- Competition

From there, you can start sorting and filtering your keywords based on the criteria that are most important to you. For example, you might want to focus on keywords with high search volume and low competition. Or, you might want to focus on keywords that are relevant to your business but have low search volume. It all depends on your priorities and what you're trying to achieve with your SEO campaign.

Example strategies:

1. If you want to increase traffic to your website

   - Identify keywords with high search volume and low competition.

2. If you want to improve conversions from search traffic

   - Identify long-tail keywords with low competition that indicate the desired intent, for example, if you sell cat toys, you might want to target the keyword "buy cat toys online."

3. If you want to build links

    – Identify keywords with an informational intent that
      trigger a featured snippet, for example, "How to...,"
      "What is...," etc.

4. If you want to create brand awareness

    – Identify keywords with high click-through rates but
      low competition.

Once you've evaluated your keywords, it's time to start organizing
them. There are a few different ways you can do this:

–   Create a keyword map: This is a visual representation of
    how your keywords are related to each other. It can be
    helpful to create a keyword map before you start
    writing content, so you have a clear idea of what topics
    you want to cover.

–   Group keywords by topic: This is a simple way to
    organize your keywords into different categories. For
    example, you might want to group all of your keywords
    related to "cat toys" into one category, and all of your
    keywords related to "cat food" into another.

–   Prioritize your keywords: Once you've grouped your
    keywords by topic, you can start prioritizing which ones
    you want to target first. This can be based on a variety
    of factors, such as search volume, competition, or
    relevance to your business.

Additionally, you might want to group keywords by intent. This can be
helpful if you want to create different types of content for different stages
of the buyer's journey. For example, you might want to group all of your
keywords that have a transactional intent (such as "buy cat toys online")

into one category, and all of your keywords that have an informational intent (such as "how to take care of a cat") into another.

There are four main types of intent: navigational (people who want to go directly to a specific website), commercial (people who want to buy something), informational (people who want to learn something), and transactional (people who want to do something). Checking intent is relatively simple; all you need to do is type your keyword into Google and see what type of results come up. If most of the results are website listings, then the intent behind that keyword is probably navigational. If most of the results are from educational sites like Wikipedia or YouTube videos, then the intent behind that keyword is probably informational. If most of the results are from ecommerce sites, then the intent behind that keyword is probably transactional.

Key Takeaways

Keyword research is an essential part of any effective SXO strategy and can help you identify new content opportunities, improve your search rankings, and drive more traffic to your website. By using these methods and tools, you can find the right keywords that your target audience is searching for and optimize your content to meet their needs.

Some key takeaways from this section include

- Keyword research is essential for finding new content opportunities.

- Brainstorming with different teams can lead to a comprehensive list of potential keywords that you might not have thought of on your own.

- Trending keyword research using Google Trends can help you identify the kinds of terms people are searching for right now and what topics are popular.

- Evergreen keyword research is important for sustainable growth in traffic and leads throughout the year.

- Competitor keyword research can help you identify the keywords your competitors are targeting and analyze their keyword strategies, rankings, and search traffic.

Optimizing Website's Structure

When it comes to SXO, most people focus on the content of their website. However, the structure of your website is just as important when it comes to SXO. In fact, if your website is not properly structured, then your content will not be able to reach its full potential. In this section, we will discuss the importance of website structure for SXO and how you can improve the structure of your website for better results.

What Is Website Structure?

Website structure refers to the way in which the pages on your website are organized and linked together. For example, if you have a website with five pages, then the structure of your website would be determined by how those five pages are linked together.

The structure of your website is important for two main reasons:

1) It helps search engines understand your website: Search engines use web crawlers to index websites and determine their ranking in search results. Web crawlers follow links to find new pages, and they use the structure of a website to understand the relationships between different pages. For example, if you have a page about SEO that is linked to from your home page, then that page will be given more

weight than a page about SEO that is not linked to from any other page on your site. This is because the link from your home page tells the web crawler that the page about SEO is important and should be given a higher ranking in search results.

2) It helps visitors navigate your website: The structure of your website also determines how easy it is for visitors to find the information they are looking for on your site. If your website is properly structured, then visitors will be able to easily navigate from one page to another and find the information they need. However, if your website is not properly structured, then visitors will get lost and leave your site without finding the information they need.

How to Improve the Structure of Your Website

There are a number of elements that contribute to a website's structure, including the navigation menu, footer, and URL structure. Each of these elements plays an important role in how easy it is for visitors to find the information they are looking for on your website. In addition, each of these elements can also influence your website's search engine optimization (SEO) and conversion rates (CRO). As such, it is important to take the time to consider what works best for both your visitors and your business when planning the structure of your website.

Navigation Menu

The navigation menu is one of the most important aspects of your website's structure. It allows visitors to easily find their way around your site and access the information they are looking for.

There are a few things to keep in mind when designing your navigation menu, including

- Keep it simple: The navigation menu should be easy to understand and use. Visitors should be able to find their way around your site without getting frustrated.

- Organize items logically: The navigation menu should be organized in a way that makes sense for both visitors and search engines. Group items together that are related and consider using labels that accurately describe the content on each page.

- Use drop-down menus sparingly: Drop-down menus can be helpful for organizing large websites with lots of content, but they can also be confusing for visitors if they are used too frequently. If possible, try to stick with a simple top-level navigation menu.

Footer

The footer is another important element of your website's structure. The footer typically contains links to important pages on your site, such as your contact information, privacy policy, terms of service, etc. In addition, the footer is also a good place to include social media buttons and links to your blog or newsletter.

When designing your footer, there are a few things to keep in mind:

- Keep it simple: Like the navigation menu, the footer should be easy to understand and use. Stick to the essential links and buttons that visitors will need.

- Use whitespace: Don't feel like you need to cram everything into the footer. Use whitespace to separate different sections so that it is easy for visitors to scan through the footer and find what they are looking for.

– Make it responsive: With more people accessing websites from mobile devices than ever before, it is important to make sure that your footer looks good on all screen sizes. This includes using larger font sizes and buttons that are easy to tap on smaller screens.

Page Titles

The title of each page on your website plays an important role in both SEO and CRO. The title should accurately reflect the content on the page while also containing keywords that you want to rank for in search engines. In addition, attention-grabbing titles can also help increase click-through rates from SERPs (search engine results pages).

– Keep it short and sweet: Page titles should be short enough so that they can be easily read and understood by both humans and search engines. Aim for 50–60 characters or less whenever possible.

– Use keyword phrases: When possible, try to include keyword phrases rather than single keywords in your page titles. This will help improve your chances of ranking in SERPs while also making it clear what each page is about at a glance.

– Be descriptive: In addition to including keywords, page titles should also be descriptive. This will help visitors understand what the page is about before they even click through.

Header Tags

In addition to the title of each page, the header tags (H1–H6) are also important for both SEO and CRO. The main H1 tag should be used to describe the content on the page, while the other H2–H6 tags can be used to highlight important subheadings.

- Use keyword phrases: Just like with page titles, it is important to include keyword phrases in your header tags whenever possible. This will help improve your chances of ranking in SERPs while also making it clear what each page is about at a glance.

- Be descriptive: In addition to including keywords, header tags should also be descriptive. This will help visitors understand what the page is about before they even click through.

URL Structure

The URL (uniform resource locator) structure of each page on your website plays an important role in both SEO and usability. URLs should be short, descriptive, and easy to understand. In addition, they should also use keyword phrases whenever possible.

- Keep it simple: The ideal URL structure is short, descriptive, and easy to understand. Avoid using special characters whenever possible. It's also important to use dashes ("-") instead of underscores ("_") in your URLs. Search engines generally view dashes as word separators, whereas underscores are seen as part of the same word.

- Use keyword phrases: When possible, try to include keyword phrases rather than single keywords in your URLs. This will help improve your chances of ranking in SERPs while also making it clear what each page is about at a glance. For example, instead of using a URL like "`www.example.com/products?id=123`", you could use a more descriptive URL like "`www.example.com/luxury-handbags`". This not only includes a relevant keyword phrase but also gives users a better idea of what they can expect to find on that page.

Anchor Text

The anchor text is the actual text that is used to link to other pages on your website. The anchor text plays an important role in both SEO and usability. Anchor text should be descriptive and relevant to the page it is linking to. In addition, it should also use keyword phrases whenever possible.

- Keep it relevant: The anchor text should be relevant to the page it is linking to. Avoid using generic phrases like "click here" or "learn more" whenever possible.

- Use keyword phrases: When possible, try to include keyword phrases rather than single keywords in your anchor text. This will help improve your chances of ranking in SERPs while also making it clear what each page is about at a glance.

Internal Linking Structure

The internal linking structure of your website plays an important role in both SEO and usability. Internal links should be used to link to other pages on your website in a way that is relevant and helpful to users.

- Keep it relevant: Internal links should be used to link to other pages on your website in a way that is relevant and helpful to users. Avoid linking for the sake of linking.

- Use keyword phrases: When possible, try to include keyword phrases rather than single keywords in your internal links. This will help improve your chances of ranking in SERPs while also making it clear what each page is about at a glance.

Sitemap

A sitemap is an important tool for both SEO and usability. A sitemap is a list of all the pages on your website that is designed to help users and search engines find what they are looking for.

- Include all pages: Be sure to include all pages on your website in your sitemap. This will help search engines index your website more thoroughly and make it easier for users to find what they are looking for.

Schema Markup

Schema markup is a code that you can add to your website to help search engines understand the content on your pages. This can be used to provide additional information about products, services, events, and more. In addition, schema markup can also be used to improve the way your listings appear in SERPs.

Key Takeaways

Website structure is just as important as content when it comes to SXO. A well-structured website can help search engines understand your site better, and it can also help visitors navigate your site and find the information they need.

Some key takeaways from this section include

- Website structure refers to the organization and linking of website pages, which is important for search engine understanding and visitor navigation.

- Elements that contribute to website structure include the navigation menu, footer, URL structure, page titles, header tags, anchor text, internal linking structure, sitemap, and schema markup.

- To improve website structure, keep the navigation menu and footer simple, use whitespace and larger font sizes, and make sure the footer looks good on all screen sizes.

- When designing page titles, keep them short and descriptive, use keyword phrases, and make them attention-grabbing.

- Use header tags (H1–H6) to highlight important subheadings and include keyword phrases whenever possible.

- For URL structure, keep it simple, descriptive, and easy to understand, use dashes instead of underscores, and include keyword phrases.

- Anchor text should be descriptive, relevant, and use keyword phrases whenever possible.

- Internal links should be relevant and helpful to users and use keyword phrases whenever possible.

- A sitemap is a list of all the pages on your website that is designed to help users and search engines find what they are looking for.

- Schema markup is a code that you can add to your website to help search engines understand the content on your pages and improve the way your listings appear in SERPs.

Summary

- Analyzing the website's current search experience is the first step to improve it. Use various tools like Google Analytics and Microsoft Clarity to gather data and understand user behavior.

- Identifying the target audience is important for developing a targeted SXO strategy. Gather customer insights from various sources like feedback questionnaires and social listening to create a customer persona.

- Keyword research is essential to identify new content opportunities and improve search rankings. Use methods like brainstorming and competitor research to find the right keywords for your website.

- Website structure is important for search engine understanding and visitor navigation. Consider elements like the navigation menu, footer, URL structure, and internal linking structure to improve it.

CHAPTER 3

Creating Compelling Content

If you want your site to be successful, you need to create content that is compelling and useful for both users and search engines. In this chapter, we'll discuss the different types of content that work well for SXO. We'll cover the different purposes of each type of content, such as establishing thought leadership, providing helpful information to potential customers, or moving visitors further down the marketing funnel. By the end of this chapter, you should have a good understanding of which types of content will work best for your SXO strategy.

Types of Content That Work Well for SXO

There are many different types of content that can be effective for SXO. The best type of content for your website will depend on your business goals and your audience.

© Zuzanna Krüger 2023
Z. Krüger, *The Art of SXO*, Design Thinking, https://doi.org/10.1007/978-1-4842-9212-9_3

Industry News and Insights

Industry news and insights can be used to establish thought leadership. This type of content showcases your company's expertise on a given topic and helps build trust with potential customers. It can also be used to keep your existing customers up to date on industry trends. Industry news and insights typically take the form of

- – Blog posts
- – Articles
- – Whitepapers
- – Infographics

Audience-Focused Content

Audience-focused content is all about providing helpful information to your target market. This type of content is usually more general in nature than industry news and insights, but it still needs to be relevant to your target market's interests. Audience-focused content can take many different forms, such as

- – Ebooks
- – Guides
- – FAQs

Marketing Funnel Stage-Specific Content

Marketing funnel stage-specific content is designed to move visitors further down the marketing funnel toward conversion. This type of content is usually more sales-oriented than the other two types. It aims to educate potential customers about your products or services and convince them to buy from you. Marketing funnel stage-specific content can include things like

- Product demos

- Webinars

- Free trials/samples

- Case studies

Now that we've covered the different types of content that work well for SXO, let's take a closer look at each content piece.

Blog Posts

Blog posts are a great way to share your company's insights on a given topic. They can be used to educate your target market about your industry, showcase your company's expertise, and build trust with potential customers. In addition, blog posts can also be used to keep your existing customers up to date on industry trends.

Articles

Articles are similar to blog posts, but they tend to be more in depth and comprehensive. They are a great way to establish thought leadership and build trust with potential customers. You may use articles to keep your existing customers informed about market changes.

Whitepapers

Whitepapers are long-form pieces of content that are usually highly technical in nature. They can be used to showcase your company's expertise on a given subject. Whitepapers are typically used as lead generation tool, so they should include a call to action (CTA) that encourages visitors to sign up for your email list or download a freebie in exchange for their contact information.

Ebooks

Ebooks are long-form pieces of content that provide helpful information to your target market. They can be used to educate potential customers about your products or services, convince them to buy from you, or move them further down the marketing funnel.

Guides

Guides are similar to ebooks, but they tend to be shorter and more to the point. They can be used to educate potential customers about your products or services, convince them to buy from you, or move them further down the marketing funnel.

FAQs

FAQs are a great way to provide helpful information to your target market. They can be used to answer common questions about your industry, product, or service. FAQs can also be used to generate organic traffic from long-tail keywords.

Product Demos

Product demos are an excellent way to showcase your products or services in action. They usually take the form of a video or an interactive tool, and they are used lower down in the marketing funnel to convince potential customers to purchase your products.

Webinars

Webinars are online seminars that you can use to educate your target market about your products or services. They usually include a presentation followed by a Q&A session. Webinars can be used to generate leads, build trust with potential customers, and increase brand awareness.

Free Trials/Samples

Free trials or samples are an excellent way to let potential customers experience your products or services firsthand. In many cases, customers are more likely to buy from you after they've had a chance to try out your products or services.

Case Studies

Case studies are in-depth accounts of how your products or services have helped solve real-world problems for your customers. They are an excellent way to showcase the results that your products or services can achieve, and they can also be used to generate leads.

What to consider before choosing which content pieces to create

There are a few key elements that you'll need to consider when creating your strategy:

- Your target audience: Who are you trying to reach with your content?

- Your goals: What do you hope to achieve with your content?

- Your budget: How much money are you willing to spend on content creation?

- Your timeline: When do you want to publish your content?

- Your distribution channels: How will you promote your content?

- Your metrics: How will you measure the success of your content?

When creating your content strategy, it's important to keep your target audience in mind. You'll need to create content that appeals to them and addresses their needs. You should also consider your goals for creating content. Are you looking to generate leads? Drive traffic to your website? Increase brand awareness?

Formatting Your Content for Users and Search Engines

In this chapter, we're going to deep dive into the world of content formatting and show you how to format your content for maximum value. We'll cover how to format your content for readability, shareability, accessibility, and localization.

Formatting Your Content for Readability

One of the most important aspects of content formatting is readability. Readability refers to how easy it is for your target audience to read and understand your content. When formatting your content for readability, there are a few key elements that you'll need to keep in mind:

- Use short paragraphs: Breaking your content up into short paragraphs makes it easier to read and digest.

- Use clear and simple language: Write in a clear and concise manner using simple language. Avoid jargon and technical terms.

- Use headlines and subheadlines: Use headlines and subheadlines to break up your content and make it easier to scan.

- Use bullet points and lists: Bullet points and lists are easy to read and can help highlight key information.

- Use images and videos: Adding images and videos to your content can help break up the text and make it more visually appealing.

Formatting Your Content for Shareability

Another important aspect of content formatting is shareability. Shareability refers to how easy it is for your target audience to share your content with their networks. When formatting your content for shareability, there are a few key elements that you'll need to keep in mind:

- Make your content shareable: Include social sharing buttons on your content so that it can be easily shared on social media.

- Optimize your images and videos: Optimize your images and videos for social media platforms like Facebook, Twitter, and Pinterest.

- Include a call to action: Include a call to action in your content to encourage your readers to share it.

Formatting Your Content for Accessibility

Another important aspect of content formatting is accessibility. Accessibility refers to how easy it is for people with disabilities to access and consume your content. When formatting your content for accessibility, there are a few key elements that you'll need to keep in mind:

- Use alternative text: Alternative text is used to describe images and videos for people who are unable to see them.

- Transcribe audio and video: Transcribing audio and video files makes them accessible to people who are deaf or hard of hearing.

- Caption videos: Adding captions to videos makes them accessible to people who are deaf or hard of hearing.

- Provide transcripts: Providing transcripts of audio and video files makes them accessible to people who are deaf or hard of hearing.

Formatting Your Content for Localization

Another important aspect of content formatting is localization. Localization refers to tailoring your content to a specific geographic region or cultural group. When formatting your content for localization, there are a few key elements that you'll need to keep in mind:

- Translate your content: If you're targeting a global audience, you'll need to translate your content into multiple languages.

– Consider cultural differences: Be aware of cultural differences when formatting your content for localization. For example, avoid using sensitive words or phrases that could be offensive to certain groups.

– Use local references: Use local references in your content to appeal to your target audience. For example, if you're targeting a Spanish-speaking audience, you could use local Spanish slang or references to popular Spanish culture.

Formatting Your Content for Search Engine Optimization

1. Use keyword-rich titles and descriptions

   The title and meta description are some of the first things users see when your website appears in SERPs—so it's important to make sure they're keyword-rich and accurately reflect the content on your page. Not only will this help users decide whether to click through to your website, but it will also signal to search engines what your page is about, helping you rank higher for relevant searches.

2. Format your headings and subheadings with HTML tags

   Headings and subheadings are crucial for helping users skim-read your content and understand its structure; they act as chapters of a book. They also give search engines an idea of what your page is about. As such, it's important to format them using

HTML tags (e.g., H1 for headings, H2 for sections, and H3 for subsections). Not only will this make your content more user-friendly, but it will also help improve your SEO.

3. Use bullet points and whitespace liberally

No one wants to read huge walls of text—not even Google's bots! So make sure to break up your content using bullet points, whitespace, and other visual elements like images and infographics. Not only will this make your content easier to read, but it will also help improve its chances of ranking high in SERPs.

4. Incorporate keywords naturally into your content

Including keywords throughout your content is essential for ranking high in SERPs—but beware of keyword stuffing! Search engines are sophisticated enough to detect when you're cramming too many keywords into your content, which can result in penalties or demotions in SERP rankings. Instead, focus on incorporating keywords naturally into your sentences and paragraphs.

5. Optimize your images

Whenever you upload a photo or other image to your website, make sure to optimize it for SEO purposes. That means giving it a relevant file name (e.g., "red-leather-boots.jpg") and adding ALT text—a short description of the image that helps Google index it properly—to each one before publishing it on your site. You can also improve your image SEO by compressing your images to reduce their file size without sacrificing quality. Doing so will help your pages load faster, which is another ranking factor Google takes into account.

6. Implement schema markup

Schema markup is a code that you can add to your website to help search engines understand its content better. By implementing schema markup, you can give search engines specific information about your business, such as your address, phone number, operating hours, and more. This can help your website appear in SERPs with rich snippets—additional information that appears beneath your listing, like reviews or pricing.

Writing Effective Calls to Action

Your CTA is what tells your website visitors what you want them to do next—whether that's signing up for your newsletter, downloading a whitepaper, or making a purchase. An effective CTA is clear, concise, and, above all else, relevant to your target audience.

What Is a CTA?

A CTA is a short statement that tells your website visitors what you want them to do next. CTAs can be found anywhere on your website where you want to encourage your visitors to take action—most commonly in the form of a button or link. They can be as simple as "sign up now" or "learn more," or they can be more creative and detailed. However, no matter what form they take, all effective CTAs have one thing in common: they are relevant to their target audience.

137

How to Write an Effective CTA

There are four key elements of an effective CTA: conciseness, clarity, relevancy, and urgency. Let's break each of these down in more detail:

1. Conciseness: A good CTA should be short and sweet. Users shouldn't have to read through paragraphs of text before they understand what you want them to do next. Be direct and use active language; for example, instead of saying "click here," say "sign up now."

2. Clarity: It should be immediately clear to users what will happen when they click your CTA. Will they be taken to another page on your website? Will they be prompted to enter their contact information? Make sure it's abundantly clear so that there's no confusion or ambiguity.

3. Relevancy: As we mentioned before, relevancy is key when it comes to writing an effective CTA. Your CTAs should always be relevant to the products/ services you're selling as well as the needs/wants of your target audience. For example, if you're selling skincare products, your CTA might say "find the perfect moisturizer for your skin type." This speaks directly to users who are looking for skincare advice and helps them understand how your product can solve their problem—making them more likely to convert.

4. Urgency: Including a sense of urgency in your CTAs can also help increase conversions. Try using words like "now," "today," or "instant"—anything that conveys a sense of immediacy without coming across as too pushy or salesy. Just remember not to overdo it; too much urgency can have the opposite effect and turn users away from your website entirely.

Creating Visuals That Help Users Understand Your Content

Visuals play an important role in web design for a variety of reasons. First and foremost, they help break up text and make your content more visually appealing. They can also help illustrate complex concepts, making them easier for users to understand. And finally, visuals can help add personality to your website and make it more memorable for users.

When used effectively, visuals can have a positive impact on user engagement, time on site, and even conversion rates. However, it's important to use visuals sparingly and only when they genuinely add value to your content; otherwise, they can clutter your page and actually detract from the user experience.

When creating visuals for your website, there are a few things to keep in mind:

- Think about what you want to communicate with your visual. What is the main point you want to get across?

- Consider what type of visual will best communicate your message. A graph may be best for some messages, while a photo or infographic may be better for others.

- Make sure the visual is high quality and free of any typos or errors.

- Ensure that the visual is properly sized and placed on the page so that it is easy for users to find and understand.

Types of Visuals

There are many different types of visuals you can use to improve your content, including

- Images: Images are a great way to break up large blocks of text and add visual interest to your content. When selecting images for your website, be sure to choose high-quality images that are relevant to the topic at hand.

- Infographics: Infographics are a popular type of visual that can be used to communicate complex information in an easy-to-understand format. When creating an infographic, be sure to use clear and concise text, as well as strong visuals that complement the information you're trying to communicate.

- Charts and graphs: Charts and graphs are another effective way to communicate complex information in a visual format. When using charts and graphs on your website, be sure to choose those that are easy to understand and interpret. You may also want to include a legend or key so that users can easily understand what they're looking at.

- Videos: Videos are a great way to add visual interest to your website while also providing users with valuable information. When selecting videos for your website, be sure to choose those that are high quality and relevant to the topic at hand. You should also consider transcribing the video for users who are unable or unwilling to watch it.

The best type of visual for your website will depend on your specific goals and objectives. For example, if you're trying to increase brand awareness, using images or infographics with your logo or branding can be a good way to do this. If you're trying to sell a product, however, using product photos or videos might be more effective.

Choosing the Right Visuals

When choosing visuals for your website, it's important to keep three things in mind: relevancy, context, and aesthetics.

1. Relevancy: First and foremost, your visuals should be relevant to your target audience and the products/services you're selling. Remember that people are visual creatures; they're much more likely to remember your brand if they can see it in a relevant context.

2. Context: It's also important to make sure that your visuals are placed in the right context on your website. For example, if you're selling a product, you'll want to use high-quality photos of that product (or video if you have it) on your product page. People should be able to see what they're buying before they make a purchase.

3. Aesthetics: Finally, your visuals should be aesthetically pleasing and professional. This doesn't mean that they need to be perfect—in fact, sometimes imperfections can add character and appeal—but they should look like they belong on your website. Using visuals that are too low quality or out of date will make your website look unprofessional and could turn users away.

Key Takeaways

Creating compelling content is an essential aspect of a successful SXO strategy. By understanding the different types of content that work well for SXO and how to format your content for both users and search engines, you can create content that resonates with your target audience and drives traffic to your website. Remember to consider your audience, goals, budget, timeline, distribution channels, and metrics when creating your content strategy, and focus on incorporating keywords and optimizing your content for maximum value.

Some key takeaways from this section include

- To be successful, your website needs to have compelling and useful content for both users and search engines.

- The types of content that work well for SXO include industry news and insights, audience-focused content, and marketing funnel stage-specific content.

- When choosing which content pieces to create, consider your target audience, goals, budget, timeline, distribution channels, and metrics.

- Formatting your content for readability, shareability, accessibility, localization, and search engine optimization (SEO) is crucial for success.

- To format your content for readability, use short paragraphs, clear and simple language, headlines and subheadlines, bullet points and lists, and images and videos.

- To format your content for shareability, make it shareable, optimize images and videos, and include a call to action.

- To format your content for accessibility, use alternative text, transcribe audio and video, caption videos, and provide transcripts.

- To format your content for localization, translate it, consider cultural differences, and use local references.

- To format your content for SEO, use keyword-rich titles and descriptions, format headings and subheadings with HTML tags, use bullet points and whitespace liberally, incorporate keywords naturally into your content, optimize your images, and implement schema markup.

- A CTA is a short statement that tells website visitors what action to take next, and an effective CTA is clear, concise, and relevant to the target audience.

- An effective CTA has four key elements: conciseness, clarity, relevancy, and urgency.

- Visuals can break up text, make content more visually appealing, and help illustrate complex concepts, but should be used sparingly and only when they add value to the content.

- When creating visuals, consider what message you want to communicate and what type of visual will best communicate the message, and ensure that the visual is high quality, properly sized, and easy for users to find and understand.

- Different types of visuals that can be used include images, infographics, charts and graphs, and videos, and the best type of visual for your website will depend on your goals and objectives.

- When choosing visuals, keep in mind relevancy, context, and aesthetics, and ensure that the visuals are relevant to the target audience and products/services being sold, placed in the appropriate context on the website, and aesthetically pleasing and professional.

Improving Website Design and Functionality

Your website's design and functionality play a big role in SXO. A well-designed website that's easy to navigate and use will help improve your SEO, CRO, and UX—all of which are essential for online success.

Creating a Responsive Design

One of the most important design elements to consider when optimizing your website is responsiveness. In today's mobile-first world, it's essential that your website is designed to work well on all devices—from desktop computers to tablets to smartphones.

There are a few key things to keep in mind when creating a responsive design:

- Use responsive templates: If you're using a content management system (CMS)[1] like WordPress or Drupal, there are responsive templates available that can make creating a responsive design much easier.

- Optimize your images: Make sure your images are properly sized for different devices. You don't want them to be too large or small.

- Use media queries: Media queries are a CSS3[2] feature that allows you to create different stylesheets for different devices. This is a great way to make sure your website looks its best on all devices.

---

[1] CMS (content management system) is a software application or platform used to create, manage, and publish digital content, such as websites, blogs, and online stores. CMS allows users to create and edit content without requiring advanced technical skills, as it typically provides a user-friendly interface and a range of tools and templates for creating and customizing web pages. CMS can be used to manage a variety of content types, such as text, images, videos, and multimedia. Some popular CMS platforms include WordPress, Drupal, and Joomla, which are open source software programs that can be customized and extended by developers.

[2] CSS3 (Cascading Style Sheets 3) is the latest version of the CSS standard, which is used to style and format web pages and user interfaces. CSS3 includes a range of new features and improvements over earlier versions of the CSS standard, such as new selectors, properties, and functions for styling text, layout, and visual effects. Some of the most notable features of CSS3 include border radius, box shadow, media queries, and web fonts. CSS3 is widely used in web development to create responsive and visually appealing web pages and is supported by all modern web browsers.

    −   Test, test, test: Always test your responsive design on different devices before launch. This will help you identify any potential problems so you can fix them before your website goes live.

Implementing an Effective Navigation

Your website's navigation is also important for SXO purposes. A well-designed navigation will help improve your SEO by making it easier for search engines to index your website's content. It will also help improve your UX by making it easier for users to find what they're looking for on your website.

There are a few key things to keep in mind when creating an effective navigation:

1. Use clear and concise labels

    Your navigation labels should be clear and concise so that users can easily understand what each link leads to. This is especially important if you have a lot of content on your website. Typically, it's best to use one- or two-word labels, for example, "Products," "Services," etc. Some of the most common navigation labels are

    - Home

    - About Us

    - Products/Services

    - Blog

    - Contact Us

By using commonly understood labels, you can make it easier for users to find their way around your website and improve your website's UX.

2. Group similar items together

    When possible, try to group similar items together in your navigation. This will help users find what they're looking for more easily and reduce user friction. For example, if you have a website that sells both products and services, you might want to create two separate navigation items: "Products" and "Services." This way, users can easily find what they're looking for without having to search through a long list of items or a wall of text.

3. Use drop-down menus only when necessary

    Drop-down menus can be helpful if you have a lot of content on your website, but they should be used sparingly. This is because they can often be confusing and difficult to use. If possible, it's best to stick to a simple navigation with links that lead directly to the content you want users to see. This will help to reduce user friction and make it easier for users to find what they're looking for instead of getting frustrated and leaving your website. If you need to use drop-down menus, avoid using more than two levels.

4. Use breadcrumbs

Breadcrumbs are a type of navigation that helps users understand their location on your website. They're typically displayed as a series of links, with the current page being the last link in the series. For example:

Home ➤ Products ➤ Product A

Breadcrumbs can be helpful for users who are trying to find their way around a website with a lot of content, especially on ecommerce sites. They can also be helpful for SEO purposes, as they help search engines understand the structure of your website and index your content more effectively.

5. Include a search bar

A search bar is another important element for both SEO and UX purposes. It allows users to quickly and easily find the content they're looking for on your website without having to navigate through numerous menu items or pages. This can be especially helpful if you have a lot of content or if your website's navigation is complex.

6. Make sure your navigation is mobile-friendly

It's important to make sure that your website's navigation is mobile-friendly. This is because more and more users are accessing the Internet from mobile devices.

According to Statista, in 2022, 59.6% of website traffic comes from mobile devices. This number is only going to continue to grow in the years to come.[3]

Therefore, it's important to make sure that your website's navigation is responsive and can be easily used on mobile devices. This includes making sure that your menu items are easy to tap on a small screen and that your search bar is easily accessible.

7. Test your navigation

    Always test your navigation on different devices before launch. This will help you identify any potential problems so you can fix them before your website goes live. Additionally, it's a good idea to test your navigation periodically to make sure that it's still working well and that there haven't been any changes that could impact its usability.

8. Use analytics to track user behavior

    Analytics can be helpful for understanding how users are interacting with your website's navigation. This information can be used to improve the navigation and make it more user-friendly.

---

[3] Statista. (2022). Global mobile traffic 2022 | Statista. [online] Available at www.statista.com/statistics/277125/share-of-website-traffic-coming-from-mobile-devices/ [Accessed Feb. 20, 2023].

Some things you might want to track include

- The number of clicks on each menu item

- The average time spent on each page

- The number of visitors who abandon your website after trying to use the navigation

9. Keep your navigation simple

When it comes to website navigation, simplicity is key. You want to make sure that your navigation is easy to use and understand. This means avoiding anything that could confuse or frustrate users.

Some things to avoid include

- Using complex language or jargon

- Making menu items too small or difficult to click

- Hiding important information in drop-down menus

10. Get feedback from users

One of the best ways to improve your website's navigation is to get feedback from actual users. You can do this by conducting usability tests or surveys. This will give you valuable insights into what users like and don't like about your website's navigation and what changes you need to make.

Improving Usability with UX Design Principles

There are a number of UX design principles that can be used to improve the usability of a website. These principles can be used to help guide the design process, and they can be used to evaluate the effectiveness of a design.

Some of the most important UX design principles include

- Usability: A website should be easy to use, and it should meet the needs of the user.

- Flexibility: A website should be flexible, so that it can be used in different ways. It should be able to adapt to the needs of the user.

- Simplicity: A website should be simple, so that it is easy to use. The design should be uncluttered, and the user should be able to find what they are looking for easily.

- Learnability: A website should be easy to learn, so that users can quickly learn how to use it. The user interface should be intuitive, and users should be able to quickly learn how to navigate the site.

- Visibility: A website should be easy to see, so that users can find what they are looking for. The design should be easy to read, and the user should be able to see all of the content that is on the page.

- Consistency: A website should be consistent, so that users can easily use it. The design should be consistent, and the user interface should be consistent across all pages.

- Feedback: A website should provide feedback, so that users can know what they are doing wrong or right. Feedback should be immediate, so that users can quickly learn from their mistakes.

How can you use these UX design principles to improve the usability of your website?

Make It Easy to Use

One of the most important principles of good UX design is to keep things simple. This means avoiding anything that could confuse or frustrate users.

Some things to avoid include

- Using too much technical jargon

- Including too many steps in a process

- Making it difficult to find what users are looking for

An example of this principle in action is the Amazon.com website. Amazon.com is known for its simple and easy-to-use interface. Users can find what they are looking for quickly and easily without any frustration. Let's take a closer look:

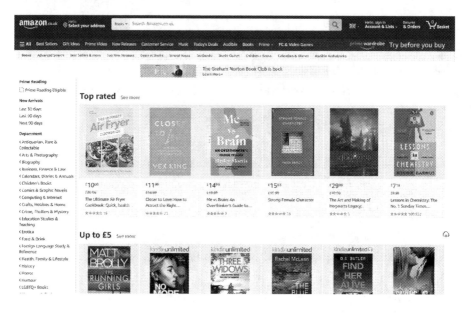

Ease of Use

One of the most important aspects of any ecommerce site is ease of use. Users should be able to find what they're looking for quickly and easily without any frustration. Amazon's UX design team has done an excellent job of keeping things simple and easy to use. The interface is clean and uncluttered, and users can easily find what they're looking for using the search bar or the navigation menu.

Search Bar

The search bar is prominently displayed at the top of every page on Amazon, making it easy for users to find what they're looking for. The search bar also autocompletes queries as you type, which makes it even easier to find what you're looking for.

Navigation Menu

The navigation menu is located on the left side of every page on Amazon. It includes links to all of the main sections of the site, such as "Shop by Department," "Today's Deals," and "Customer Service." The navigation menu is easy to use and navigate, and it allows users to quickly find what they're looking for.

Product Pages

Amazon's product pages are well-designed and provide all of the information that users need to make a purchase decision. The product image is prominently displayed, and users can easily view additional images by clicking the arrows under the main image. The product title, price, customer reviews, and other important information are all clearly displayed, making it easy for users to find what they're looking for. Additionally, users can easily add products to their shopping cart or wish list by clicking the buttons below the product image.

One-Click Ordering

Amazon's "one-click ordering" feature is one of the company's most popular features. It allows users to place an order with just a few clicks, without having to enter their shipping information or credit card information. This makes it easy and convenient for users to make a purchase, which is one of the reasons why Amazon is so successful.

Make It Easy to Navigate

Another important principle of good UX design is to make it easy to navigate. This means creating a logical structure that is easy to follow and providing clear labels for all of the website's pages and sections.

Some things to consider when creating an easy-to-navigate website include

- The hierarchy of the website's pages

- The order in which the pages are listed in the navigation menu

- The names of the website's pages and sections

An example of this principle in action is HubSpot.com. HubSpot has a well-organized website that is easy to navigate. The website's pages are logically organized and clearly labeled, and the navigation menu is easy to use. Let's take a closer look:

Logical Structure

HubSpot's website has a logical structure that is easy to follow. The website's pages are organized into sections, such as "Software" and "Resources." Within each section, there are subsections that are clearly labeled. For example, under the "Software" section, there are subsections for each of HubSpot's products. This makes it easy for users to find what they're looking for.

Clear Labels

All of the pages on HubSpot's website are clearly labeled. The labels are easy to read and understand, and they accurately describe the content of the pages. This makes it easy for users to find the information they're looking for.

Same CTA on Every Page

Another thing that makes HubSpot's website easy to navigate is that the call to action (CTA) is the same on every page. The CTA, "Get a demo," is prominently displayed in the top-right corner of every page. This makes it easy for users to know what they need to do next without receiving conflicting information.

Use Clear and Concise Language

Another important principle of good UX design is to use clear and concise language. This means using words that are easy to understand and avoiding jargon.

Some things to consider when using clear and concise language include

- The reading level of the text

- The clarity of the words used

- The use of slang or jargon

An example of this principle in action is Remarkable.com. Remarkable's website uses clear and concise language throughout. The text is easy to read and understand, and the words used are clear and unambiguous. Let's take a closer look:

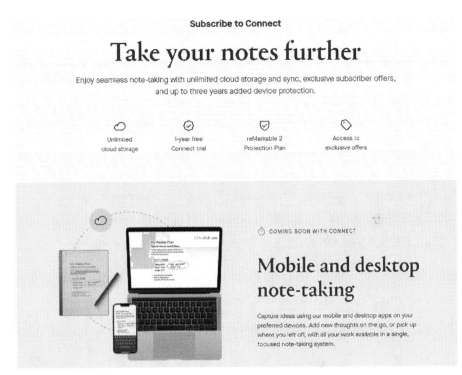

Reading Level

Remarkable's website uses language that is easy to read and understand. The reading level of the text is appropriate for users of all levels, making it accessible to everyone.

Clarity of Words Used

Remarkable's website uses clear and straightforward language. The words used are easy to understand, and they accurately describe the content of the pages. This makes it easy for users to find the information they're looking for.

Jargon-Free

Remarkable's website avoids jargon. The text is free of acronyms, abbreviations, and technical terms. This makes it easy for users to understand what they're reading.

Use Whitespace Effectively

Whitespace is the empty space on a web page that is not occupied by text or images. While it may seem like wasted space, whitespace is actually a valuable tool that can be used to improve the UX of a website.

Some things to consider when using whitespace effectively include

- The amount of whitespace on the page
- The placement of the whitespace on the page
- The use of whitespace to separate elements on the page

An example of this principle in action is Optimizely.com. Optimizely's home page uses whitespace effectively to create a clean and uncluttered look. The amount of whitespace on the page is appropriate, and the placement of the whitespace is well-balanced. Additionally, the whitespace is used to effectively separate the different elements on the page. Let's take a closer look:

Amount of Whitespace

Optimizely's home page uses an appropriate amount of whitespace. The page is not too crowded, and the whitespace helps to create a clean and uncluttered look.

Placement of Whitespace

The whitespace on Optimizely's home page is well-balanced. It is used to effectively separate the different elements on the page, and it does not overwhelm the content.

159

Use of Whitespace to Separate Elements

Optimizely's home page uses whitespace to effectively separate the different elements on the page. The whitespace helps to create a visual hierarchy, making it easy for users to find what they're looking for.

Use Color Effectively

Color is another important element of UX design. Color can be used to create visual interest, contrast, and hierarchy. It can also be used to convey emotion and communicate messages.

Some things to consider when using color effectively include

- – The use of color in the brand identity
- – The use of color to create visual interest
- – The use of color to create contrast
- – The use of color to convey emotion
- – The use of color to communicate messages

An example of this principle in action is Lusha.com. Lusha's website uses color effectively to create visual interest and contrast. The brand identity is consistent, and the colors are used to effectively communicate messages. Let's take a closer look:

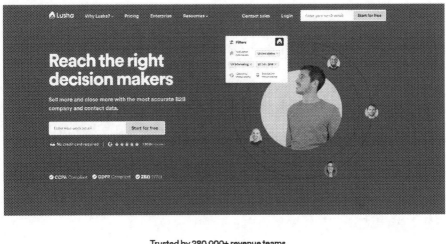

Trusted by 280,000+ revenue teams

SEISMIC   yotpo.   zendesk   aircall   airtel

Brand Identity

Lusha's website uses color consistently throughout the site. The brand identity is clear, and the colors are used to reinforce the message of the site.

Visual Interest

Lusha's website uses color to create visual interest. The colors are eye-catching and help to break up the monotony of the text.

Contrast

Lusha's website uses color to create contrast. The colors are used to highlight important information and make it easy for users to find what they're looking for.

Emotion

Lusha's website uses color to convey emotion. The colors are playful and inviting, and they help to create a positive user experience.

Communication of Messages

Lusha's website uses color to communicate messages. The colors are used to highlight important information and make it easy for users to find what they're looking for.

Use Typography Effectively

Typography is the art and technique of arranging type to make written language legible, readable, and attractive. When used effectively, typography can greatly improve the UX of a website.

Some things to consider when using typography effectively include

- The size of the text
- The typeface
- The line height
- The color of the text
- The amount of space between lines of text

An example of this principle in action is Buffer.com. Buffer's website uses typography effectively to create a clean and easy-to-read design. The size of the text is appropriate, and the typeface is easy to read. Additionally, the line height is well-balanced, and the color of the text is easy on the eyes. Let's take a closer look:

≋ Buffer　　　Tools ⌄　Channels ⌄　Pricing　Blog　　　Q Log in　[Get started now]

An assistant not a replacement

Buffer's AI Assistant is exactly what it's called. An assistant.

We want to be clear. This is not a tool that will replace creators. We don't expect the tool to remove creativity. We can't see it being used **instead** of typical human creation.

Umber, a content writer here at Buffer shared her very real concerns about AI. She talked about her unwillingness to use the new tech and her fears about how it might replace genuine, real, human creativity.

BROUGHT TO YOU BY ≋ Buffer

Try Buffer for free

140,000+ small businesses like yours use Buffer
to build their brand on social media every month

[Get started now]

Size of Text

Buffer's website uses an appropriate size for the text. The text is easy to read, and it does not overwhelm the design.

Typeface

Buffer's website uses a typeface that is easy to read. The letters are well-spaced, and the font is not too small or too large.

Line Height

Buffer's website uses a well-balanced line height. The lines of text are easy to read, and there is enough space between them.

Color of Text

Buffer's website uses a color for the text that is easy on the eyes. The text is not too bright or too dark, and it is easy to read.

Use Images Effectively

Images are an important part of any website design. They can be used to create visual interest, contrast, and emotional connection. When used effectively, images can greatly improve the UX of a website.

Some things to consider when using images effectively include

- The size of the image

- The file type of the image

- The resolution of the image

- The placement of the image

- The use of alt text

An example of this principle in action is Airbnb.com. Airbnb's website uses images effectively to create visual interest and contrast. The images are well-placed, and they help to break up the monotony of the text. Additionally, the use of alt text helps users who are unable to see the images to still understand the content. Let's take a closer look:

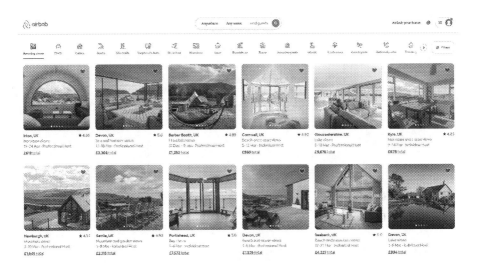

Size of Image

Airbnb's website uses images that are an appropriate size. The images are not too small or too large, and they do not overwhelm the design.

File Type of Image

Airbnb's website uses images that are in the JPEG file format. This file format is ideal for images because it is lossless, meaning that no data is lost when the image is compressed.

Resolution of Image

Airbnb's website uses images that have a resolution of 72 pixels per inch. This resolution is ideal for web images because it is low enough to load quickly, but high enough to appear sharp on most screens.

Placement of Image

Airbnb's website uses images that are well-placed. The images are used to break up the monotony of the text, and they help to guide the user's eye through the design.

Use of Alt Text

Airbnb's website uses alt text for the images. This is important for users who are unable to see the images. The alt text helps these users to still understand the content.

Use Visual Cues to Guide Users

Visual cues are an important part of any website design. They can be used to create visual interest, contrast, and emotional connection. When used effectively, visual cues can greatly improve the UX of a website.

Some things to consider when using visual cues effectively include

- The use of symbols and icons
- The use of imagery
- The use of information
- The use of buttons
- The use of color

When using visual cues, it is important to consider how they will be interpreted by the target audience. Different people will have different reactions to different visuals, so it is important to choose ones that will be effective for the specific audience you are targeting.

An example of this principle in action is Canva.com. Canva.com uses visual cues effectively to guide users through the website. The use of symbols and icons helps users to quickly understand the features, and the use of colors helps to create visual interest. The buttons are well-placed and easy to find, and the overall design is clean and uncluttered.

Use of Symbols and Icons

Canva's website uses symbols and icons to help users quickly understand the features. These symbols and icons are placed in strategic locations, and they are easy to understand.

Use of Imagery

Canva also uses imagery effectively. The images are well-chosen and help to create an emotional connection with the user.

Use of Information

The use of information is also important on Canva's website. The information is presented in a clear and concise way, and it is easy to find what you are looking for.

Use of Buttons

The buttons on Canva's website are well-placed and easy to find. They are also easy to use, and they help to guide the user through the website.

Use of Color

Color is used effectively on Canva's website. The colors are well-chosen, and they help to create visual interest.

Create Effective, Frictionless Forms

Forms are an important part of any website. They are used to collect information from users, and they can be used to improve the UX of a website.

Some things to consider when creating effective forms include

- The use of field labels

- The use of input types

- The placement of form fields

- The use of submit buttons

- The use of error messages

When creating forms, it is important to consider how they will be used by the target audience. Different people will have different needs, so it is important to create forms that are easy to use and understand.

An example of an effective form is the one used by Amazon.com. Amazon's forms are well-designed and easy to use. The field labels are clear and concise, and the input types are easy to understand. The form fields are placed in a logical order, and the submit button is easy to find.

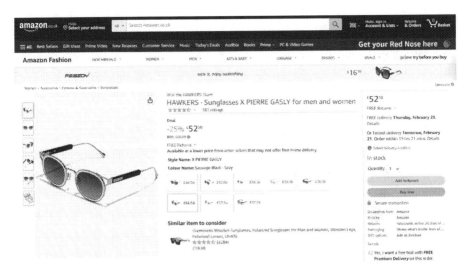

Use of Field Labels

Amazon's website uses field labels that are clear and concise. These labels help users to understand what information is being asked for.

Use of Input Types

The input types on Amazon's website are easy to understand. This makes it easy for users to fill out the form.

Placement of Form Fields

The form fields on Amazon's website are placed in a logical order. This makes it easy for users to fill out the form.

Use of Submit Buttons

The submit button on Amazon's website is easy to find. This makes it easy for users to submit the form.

Use of Error Messages

Amazon's website uses error messages that are clear and concise. These messages help users to understand what went wrong and how to fix it.

Creating a Style Guide

Once you have decided on the overall look and feel of your website, it is important to create a style guide. This will help to ensure that all of the elements on your website are consistent with each other and that other members of your team know how to use them correctly.

A style guide should include

1. Color palette

   Your color palette should be made up of a maximum of five colors. These colors should be chosen carefully to represent your brand in the best way possible. When selecting your colors, consider both the psychological effects of color as well as the technical limitations of web browsers. You will also want to make sure that your colors have enough contrast with each other so that they are accessible to people with visual impairments.

Color psychology cheat sheet:

Color	Traits
Blue	Trustworthy, professional
Red	Exciting, passionate
Yellow	Optimistic, happy
Green	Calming, refreshing
Purple	Creative, luxurious
White	Clean, simple
Black	Mysterious, powerful
Orange	Energetic, friendly

2. Typography system

   Your typography system should include two to
   three different fonts that can be used for different
   purposes. For example, you may want to use one
   font for headings and another for body text. It is
   important to consider how these fonts will work
   together and whether or not they will be compatible
   with the devices that your website will be viewed on.

   You will also want to specify which font weights
   and styles (e.g., italics) should be used in different
   situations. For example, you may want to use
   boldface for headings and regular weight for
   body text.

3. Icon system

    An icon system is a set of icons that can be used
    across your website. The icons should be designed
    in such a way that they are recognizable even when
    they are scaled down to small sizes. They should
    also be designed to work well with both light and
    dark backgrounds.

4. Grid system

    A grid system is a set of guidelines that can be used
    to position elements on your website. This system
    helps to create a sense of order on your website and
    makes it easier for people to find the information
    they are looking for. A grid system typically consists
    of 12 or 16 columns. The number of columns you
    choose will depend on the design of your website
    and the amount of content you plan on including on
    each page.

5. Button styles

    Your website will likely have several different types
    of buttons, such as submit buttons, download
    buttons, and social media buttons. It is important to
    specify the style of each type of button so that they
    are all consistent with each other.

6. Form styles

    If your website includes any forms, you will need to
    specify the style of each form element. This includes
    the style of the input fields, the submit button, and
    any error messages that may be displayed.

7. Image styles

Images are an important part of any website. They can help to break up long blocks of text and make your content more visually appealing. It is important to specify the size, shape, and file format of the images that you use on your website.

8. Video styles

If your website includes any videos, you will need to specify the size, file format, and delivery method for each video.

9. Audio styles

If your website includes any audio files, you will need to specify the file format and delivery method for each audio file.

Key Takeaways

Website design and functionality are crucial components of SXO. By creating a responsive design and implementing an effective navigation, you can improve your SEO, CRO, and UX. In addition, by following UX design principles, you can create a website that is easy to use and meets the needs of your target audience. Remember to test your website on different devices, track user behavior, and get feedback from actual users to continuously improve your website's design and functionality.

Some key takeaways from this section include

- A well-designed and functional website is essential for online success and can improve SEO, CRO, and UX.

- Creating a responsive design is important in today's mobile-first world and can be achieved through the use of responsive templates, optimized images, media queries, and testing on different devices.

- An effective navigation is important for SEO and UX and can be achieved through the use of clear and concise labels, grouping similar items, avoiding excessive use of drop-down menus, using breadcrumbs, including a search bar, making it mobile-friendly, testing, and using analytics to track user behavior.

- UX design principles such as usability, flexibility, simplicity, learnability, visibility, consistency, and feedback can be used to improve website usability.

- Creating a style guide is important to ensure consistency in website elements such as color palette, typography system, icon system, grid system, button styles, form styles, image styles, video styles, and audio styles.

Experimenting and Iterating

After you've collected some data, it's time to start experimenting. The goal of experimentation is to find the best way to achieve your desired outcome. This involves trying different things and seeing what works best.

It's important to keep in mind that there is no one perfect solution. What works for one website may not work for another. The key is to keep trying different things until you find something that works well for your particular situation.

The Importance of Experimentation

The world of online marketing is constantly changing. What works today may not work tomorrow. This is why it's so important to experiment and to always be looking for new ways to improve your website.

If you're not experimenting, you're probably not doing as well as you could be. Experimentation allows you to constantly improve your website and your digital marketing strategy. It's how you find new ways to reach your target audience and convert them into customers or clients.

The Scientific Method

One way to think about experimentation is using the scientific method. The scientific method is a process that scientists use to test hypotheses and to gather data. The steps of the scientific method are

1. Make an observation.

2. Form a hypothesis.

3. Test the hypothesis with an experiment.

4. Analyze the results of the experiment.

5. Draw a conclusion.

6. Repeat the process.

You can use the scientific method to conduct experiments on your website. Here's how it would work:

1. Make an observation: You might observe that your website's conversion rate is low or that you are not getting as much traffic as you want.

2. Form a hypothesis: You might hypothesize that changing the color of your call-to-action button will increase conversions or that adding social media buttons will increase traffic.

3. Test the hypothesis with an experiment: You would set up an A/B test to test your hypothesis.

4. Analyze the results of the experiment: You would look at the data from your A/B test to see if the change you made had the desired effect.

5. Draw a conclusion: If the results of your experiment showed that your hypothesis was correct, you would implement the change on your website. If the results showed that your hypothesis was incorrect, you would try a different change.

6. Repeat the process: You would continue experimenting until you find a change that has the desired effect on your website.

Types of Experiments

There are many different types of experiments you can run on your website. Some common types of experiments are A/B tests, multivariate tests, and user experience (UX) tests:

- A/B tests are the most common type of experiment. They involve testing two versions of a page (Version A and Version B) to see which one performs better. The version that performs better is then implemented on the website.

- Multivariate tests are similar to A/B tests, but they involve testing multiple versions of a page at the same time. This allows you to test multiple changes at once and to find the combination of changes that works best.

- User experience (UX) tests involve testing how users interact with your website. UX tests can help you identify problems with your website's design or navigation. They can also help you find ways to improve the overall user experience on your website.

How to Run an Experiment

Running an experiment is not as difficult as it might seem. There are a few simple steps you need to follow:

1. Choose the element you want to test: This could be something like the design of your website, the position of a call-to-action button, or the copy on your landing page. Typically, you will want to test one element at a time so that you can be sure that any changes in results are due to the element you are testing and not any other factors.

2. Decide on a goal for the test: This could be something like increased sales, increased web traffic, or increased time spent on your website.

3. Create two (or more) versions of the element: These versions should be different enough that you can easily tell them apart, but not so different that they are unrecognizable.

4. Choose a period of time for the test: This should be long enough to gather enough data to make a decision, but not so long that you lose interest. Typically, if you have a lot of traffic to your website, a week or two is sufficient. If you have less traffic, you may need to run the test for a month or longer.

5. Set up your test so that 50% of your visitors see Version A and 50% see Version B (or whichever version you are testing): There are a few different ways to do this, but one option is to use Google Optimize.

6. Collect data: This can be done manually by tracking the goal you chose in step 2 or automatically using a tool like Google Analytics.

7. Analyze the data: At the end of the test period, compare the results of Version A and Version B. If there is a clear winner, then you can make the decision to implement that version on your website. If the results are close, or if you are not sure which version is better, you may want to run the test for a longer period of time or try a different element.

Setting an A/B Test with Google Optimize

If you want to use Google Optimize to set up your A/B test, follow these steps:

1. Go to `https://optimize.google.com` and sign in with your Google account.

2. Click "Create Experiment."

3. Enter the URL of the page you want to test and click "Create."

4. Choose the type of experiment you want to run. For an A/B test, choose "A/B test."

5. Enter a name for your experiment and click "Next."

6. Configure the options for your experiment. For an A/B test, you will need to enter the following information:

   – The URL of Version A of the page you are testing

   – The URL of Version B of the page you are testing

   – The percentage of visitors who should see Version A (this should be 50%)

   – The percentage of visitors who should see Version B (this should be 50%)

   – The duration of the experiment

   – The objective of the experiment (what you are trying to achieve)

7. Click "Create Experiment."

8. Once the experiment is created, you will be given a piece of code to add to your website. This code should be added to the <head> section of both Version A and Version B of the page you are testing.

9. After the experiment has been running for the duration you specified, click "View Results" to see how it performed.

These are just general guidelines—you may need to adjust them depending on the specific details of your experiment.

Creating an Experimentation Road Map

After you have decided that you want to start using experimentation on your website, the next step is to create an experimentation road map. This will help you plan out which experiments you want to run and when you want to run them.

There are a few different ways to approach this:

- You can start with a list of all the possible experiments you could run and then prioritize them based on how likely they are to improve your website.

- You can start with a list of goals for your website and then brainstorm experiments that could help you achieve those goals.

- You can start with a specific problem you want to solve and then brainstorm experiments that could help you solve it.

No matter which approach you take, there are a few things you should keep in mind:

- Make sure you have enough traffic to your website before running any experiments. If you don't have enough traffic, you won't be able to get reliable results from your experiments.

- Make sure the changes you make are small. If you make too many changes at once, you won't be able to tell which change is responsible for any results you see.

- Make sure you have a plan for how you are going to track the results of your experiments. Without tracking, you won't be able to know if your experiments are successful or not.

Once you have a list of potential experiments, you can start prioritizing them. There are a few different ways to do this:

- You can prioritize based on how likely the experiment is to improve your website. This can be tricky to assess, but there are a few things you can look at to help you make a decision:

  - The complexity of the experiment: Simpler experiments are more likely to be successful than complex ones.

  - The amount of traffic you need to run the experiment: If you don't have enough traffic, you won't be able to get reliable results.

  - The amount of time and resources required to set up and run the experiment: If an experiment requires a lot of time or resources, it may not be worth doing.

- You can prioritize based on how much impact the experiment is likely to have. This can be tricky to assess, but there are a few things you can look at to help you make a decision:

  - The potential upside of the experiment: If an experiment has the potential to increase conversions by a large amount, it is more worth doing than an experiment with a smaller potential upside.

  - The downside of the experiment: If an experiment has the potential to decrease conversions by a large amount, it is less worth doing than an experiment with a smaller potential downside.

- You can prioritize based on how confident you are in the results of the experiment. This can be tricky to assess, but there are a few things you can look at to help you make a decision:

  - How well understood the problem is: If you don't fully understand the problem, it will be harder to create an experiment that solves it.

  - How well understood the solution is: If you don't fully understand the solution, it will be harder to create an experiment that tests it.

  - How much experience you have with running experiments: If you haven't run many experiments before, you may not be as confident in the results.

Once you have a list of potential experiments, you can start planning when to run them. There are a few different factors to consider when deciding when to run an experiment:

- How much traffic do you need? If you don't have enough traffic, you won't be able to get reliable results from your experiment.

- How complex is the experiment? If the experiment is complex, it will take longer to set up and run.

- How much time do you have? If you only have a limited amount of time, you may want to prioritize simpler experiments.

- How confident are you in the results? If you aren't confident in the results, you may want to wait until you have more data before making any decisions.

Once you have decided when to run your experiment, you can start planning how to run it. There are a few different factors to consider when deciding how to run an experiment:

- What is the goal of the experiment? Make sure the goal is clear before starting the experiment.

- Who is going to be involved in the experiment? Make sure everyone who needs to be involved is aware of the experiment and knows what their role is.

- What resources are required? Make sure you have all the resources you need before starting the experiment.

- How will you track the results? Make sure you have a plan for tracking the results of the experiment.

- How will you know if the experiment is successful? Make sure you have a plan for how you will know if the experiment is successful.

After you have planned your experiment, you can start setting it up. There are a few different things to consider when setting up an experiment:

- What is the control group? The control group is the group of users who will see the version of the website that isn't being changed.

- What is the test group? The test group is the group of users who will see the version of the website that is being changed.

- How big should each group be? The size of each group will depend on a number of factors, including the complexity of the experiment and the amount of traffic you have.

- How will you randomly assign users to each group? There are a few different ways to do this, but the most important thing is that each user has an equal chance of being in either group.

- How long will the experiment run for? The length of the experiment will depend on a number of factors, including the complexity of the experiment and the amount of traffic you have.

After you have set up your experiment, you can start running it. There are a few different things to consider when running an experiment:

- How often should you check the results? You should check the results regularly to see how the experiment is going.

- When should you stop the experiment? You should stop the experiment when you have enough data to make a decision or when the experiment is no longer valid.

184

- How will you know if the experiment is successful?
  Make sure you have a plan for how you will know if the
  experiment is successful.

After you have run your experiment, you can start analyzing the results.
There are a few different things to consider when analyzing the results of
an experiment:

- What were the results of the control group? The results
  of the control group will help you understand what
  would have happened without the experiment.

- What were the results of the test group? The results of
  the test group will help you understand what happened
  with the experiment.

- How do the results of the two groups compare? The
  results of the two groups will help you understand the
  impact of the experiment.

- What can you learn from the results? The results of the
  experiment will help you understand what worked and
  what didn't work.

Once you have analyzed the results of your experiment, you can start
making decisions about what to do next. There are a few different things to
consider when making decisions about an experiment:

- What did you learn from the experiment? The results of
  the experiment will help you understand what worked
  and what didn't work.

- What should you do differently next time? The results
  of the experiment will help you understand what you
  should do differently next time.

185

- What other experiments should you run? The results of the experiment will help you understand what other experiments you should run.

Key Takeaways

Experimentation and iteration are crucial components of any successful online marketing strategy. Without testing and trying out new things, it can be difficult to know what works best for your particular website and target audience. Whether you choose to run A/B tests, multivariate tests, or user experience tests, the key is to start small, track your results, and continually make improvements.

Some key takeaways from this section include

- Experimentation is an important part of online marketing, and it allows you to improve your website and digital marketing strategy continuously.

- The scientific method is a useful approach to conducting experiments on your website. It involves making an observation, forming a hypothesis, testing the hypothesis with an experiment, analyzing the results of the experiment, drawing a conclusion, and repeating the process.

- There are different types of experiments, including A/B tests, multivariate tests, and user experience (UX) tests.

- To run an experiment, you need to choose the element you want to test, decide on a goal for the test, create two or more versions of the element, choose a period of time for the test, set up the test, collect data, and analyze the data.

- To create an experimentation road map, you should prioritize experiments based on their likelihood of improving your website, their potential impact, and your confidence in the results.

- When planning and running an experiment, you need to consider factors like the goal of the experiment, the resources required, and how you will track the results.

- After running an experiment, you should analyze the results and make decisions about what to do next based on what you learned.

Reporting on SXO Success

After you have run your experiment and analyzed the results, you will need to report on your findings. There are a few different things to consider when reporting on an experiment:

1. What goals did you set for your SXO strategy?

    The first thing to consider when reporting on SXO success is what goals you set for your strategy in the first place. Without clear and measurable goals, it will be difficult to accurately assess whether or not your SXO strategy was successful. Some common goals that SXO strategies aim to achieve include improving organic search traffic, increasing conversion rates, and reducing customer churn.

2. How well did your SXO strategy achieve those goals?

    Once you've identified the goals that your SXO
    strategy was aiming to achieve, you can start to
    assess how well those goals were actually achieved.
    This can be done by looking at key metrics such
    as organic search traffic, conversion rates, and
    customer churn. If you see positive changes in these
    metrics after implementing your SXO strategy, then
    it's safe to say that your strategy was successful in
    achieving its goals.

3. What could be improved about your SXO strategy?

    Even if your SXO strategy was successful in achieving
    its goals, there's always room for improvement.
    After all, the world of SEO is constantly changing
    and evolving, so what worked today might not work
    tomorrow. Some things that you might want to
    consider improving include your keyword research,
    site architecture, and content marketing efforts.
    By continually tweaking and improving your SXO
    strategy, you can ensure that it remains effective.

4. What challenges did you face while implementing
    your SXO strategy?

    Finally, it's important to report on any challenges that
    you faced while implementing your SXO strategy.
    This can help others who are looking to implement
    similar strategies learn from your mistakes and
    avoid the same pitfalls. Some common challenges
    that people face when implementing SXO include
    dealing with resistance from stakeholders, budget
    constraints, and technical difficulties.

Choosing SXO Metrics to Track and Setting the Frequency of Your Reporting

When it comes to reporting on SXO success, there are a few different metrics that you can choose to track:

1. Conversion rate

   One of the most important things to track when measuring SXO success is your conversion rate. This metric will tell you how many people are taking the desired action on your website (such as making a purchase or signing up for a newsletter) after conducting a search. If you see a significant increase in conversion rate after implementing SXO changes, it's safe to say that your strategy is working.

2. Time on site/pages per session

   Another key metric to track is time on site/pages per session. This metric will give you an idea of how engaged users are with your website after conducting a search. If you see an increase in time on site/pages per session after implementing SXO changes, it means that users are finding what they're looking for on your website and spending more time engaging with your content.

3. Bounce rate

   Bounce rate is another important metric to consider when measuring SXO success. This metric measures the percentage of users who leave your website after viewing only one page. A high bounce rate indicates that users are not finding what they're looking for on your website and are quickly leaving. If you see a decrease in bounce rate after implementing SXO changes, it means that users are finding relevant content and sticking around longer.

4. Organic traffic

    Organic traffic is another good metric to track when measuring SXO success. This metric measures the number of visitors who come to your website from organic search results (as opposed to paid ads or other sources). If you see an increase in organic traffic after implementing SXO changes, it means that your website is ranking higher in search results and getting more visibility.

Choosing What to Include in Your SXO Report

Now that you know what metrics to track, it's time to decide what to include in your SXO report. Here are a few things to consider:

1. The current state of your website's search experience

    Before you can show how much SXO has improved your website, you need to establish a baseline of where your website's search experience was at before you made any changes. This will help others understand the magnitude of the changes that you've made and how much progress has been made.

2. The goals of your SXO strategy

   It's also important to include the goals of your SXO
   strategy in your report. This will help anyone who
   reads it understand what you were trying to achieve
   with your strategy and whether or not you were
   successful.

3. The metrics that you tracked during implementation

   As we mentioned before, there are a few different
   metrics that you can choose to track when
   measuring SXO success. Be sure to include the ones
   that you chose in your report so that your clients or
   colleagues can easily understand how your website
   performed.

4. Your recommendations for future SXO strategies

   Finally, be sure to include your recommendations
   for future SXO strategies in your report. This will
   help others understand what changes you would
   like to see made and how they can improve the
   search experience on their website.

Creating a Report Template for Future SXO Reports

Once you've created your first SXO report, it's a good idea to create a report
template that you can use for future reports. This will save you time in the
future and help you keep your reports consistent.

Here is an example report template that you can use:

1. Executive summary

   In this section, you will provide a brief overview of your report. Include the goals of your SXO strategy, the metrics that you tracked, and your overall findings.

2. The current state of your website's search experience

   In this section, you will give a rundown of your website's search experience before you made any changes. Include information on your website's structure, content, design, and any other relevant factors.

3. The goals of your SXO strategy

   In this section, you will list the goals of your SXO strategy. Be sure to include why these goals were chosen and how they align with the overall goal of improving the search experience on your website.

4. The metrics that you tracked during implementation

   In this section, you will list the metrics that you tracked during implementation. Include a brief description of each metric and how it was used to measure SXO success.

5. Results

   In this section, you will present the results of your SXO strategy. Be sure to include both positive and negative results so that others can see the full picture.

6. Your recommendations for future SXO strategies

    In this section, you will give your recommendations
    for future SXO strategies. Include information on
    what changes you would like to see made and how
    they can improve search experience on the website.

This report template can be modified to fit your specific needs and the
information that you want to include in your reports.

Key Takeaways

Reporting on SXO success is a critical step in the SXO process. It is
essential to establish clear and measurable goals, track relevant metrics,
and report on your findings to improve your website's search experience
continuously. By consistently measuring and refining your SXO strategy,
you can ensure that your website's search experience remains relevant
and engaging for your users. Use the report template provided to create
professional and consistent reports that will help you and your team stay
on track.

Some key takeaways from this section include

- To report on SXO success, it is crucial to have clear and
  measurable goals.

- Key metrics to track include conversion rate, time on
  site/pages per session, bounce rate, and organic traffic.

- It is essential to establish a baseline of your website's
  search experience, include the goals of your SXO
  strategy in your report, and track relevant metrics.

- Recommendations for future SXO strategies should be
  included in your report.

- Creating a report template can help you save time and
  maintain consistency in your reporting.

Summary

- Compelling content is essential for a successful SXO strategy. Consider different types of content and format it for readability, shareability, accessibility, localization, and SEO.

- Website design and functionality are crucial components of SXO. Create a responsive design and effective navigation, and follow UX design principles to improve usability.

- Experimentation and iteration are important for online marketing. Use A/B tests, multivariate tests, and user experience tests to improve your website and digital marketing strategy continuously.

- Reporting on SXO success is critical. Establish clear and measurable goals, track relevant metrics, and use a report template to create consistent reports.

CHAPTER 4

Advanced SXO Techniques

Once you have a basic understanding of SXO, you can start to experiment with more advanced techniques to further improve your website's search rankings and conversions. In this chapter, we will discuss five advanced SXO techniques that you can try out on your website.

International SXO

International SXO is the process of optimizing a website for international search engines. By tailoring the website's content, structure, and design to meet the needs of foreign audiences, you can improve your website's visibility and reach new markets around the world.

The Difference Between International and Multilingual SEO

One common confusion that arises when discussing international SXO is the difference between international SEO and multilingual SEO. While both international and multilingual SEO share some similarities, there are also some key differences.

© Zuzanna Krüger 2023
Z. Krüger, *The Art of SXO*, Design Thinking, https://doi.org/10.1007/978-1-4842-9212-9_4

International SEO

International SEO is all about optimizing your website for search engines in multiple countries. This means tailoring your website content, structure, and code to meet the specific requirements of each country's search engines. It's important to note that international SEO is not the same as simply translating your website into multiple languages. Rather, it's a more complex process that takes into account the different nuances of each country's search engine algorithms.

Multilingual SEO

Multilingual SEO, on the other hand, is all about optimizing your website for multiple languages. This means creating separate versions of your website for each language you want to target. Each version should be designed specifically for its target audience, with all content being translated by native speakers. Additionally, multilingual SEO requires the use of hreflang tags to ensure that search engines serve up the correct version of your website to users in each country.

Optimizing Website Structure for International Search Engines

One of the most important aspects of international SXO is optimizing the website's structure for foreign search engines. The website's structure includes both the code and the design of the site, and it plays a crucial role in how well the site ranks in foreign search engines.

Home > Top Search Engines

Search Engines Market Share

Discover the most popular search engines market share in January 2023 and over the past 12 months, quickly identify search trends and business opportunities in any region

All Platforms   Worldwide

Most Used Search Engines in January 2023

Google's market share is 91.07% in January 2023, which makes it the most popular & most used search engine in the world

Google	Bing	Yahoo	Naver	Yandex	Other
91.07%	3.00%	2.87%	0.47%	0.43%	2.16%

There are a few key things to keep in mind when optimizing the website's structure for international search engines:

1. Domain names

   When choosing a domain name for your website, it's important to consider the country or countries you're targeting. For example, if you're targeting the United States, you might want to use a .com domain name. However, if you're targeting France, you would want to use a .fr domain name.

2. Country-specific top-level domains (TLDs)

   If you're targeting multiple countries with your website, you might want to consider using country-specific top-level domains (TLDs). For example, you could use .us for the United States, .ca for Canada, and .uk for the United Kingdom. Country-specific TLDs can help improve your website's visibility in foreign search engines.

3.   HTML language tags and attributes

If you're targeting multiple languages with your website, it's important to use language tags to ensure that search engines serve up the correct version of your website to users in each language. For example, you would use the lang="en" tag for English versions of your site and the lang="fr" tag for French versions. While language tags don't have much SEO value, they allow online readers to display the correct pronunciation and accent of the web page content. Language tags also help screen readers identify the appropriate language and pronunciation, which improves accessibility for visually impaired users.

4.   Meta tags

Another important aspect of international SXO is optimizing your website's meta tags for foreign search engines. Meta tags are HTML tags that provide information about your website to search engines. There are a few different meta tags that you'll want to pay attention to when optimizing your website for foreign search engines:

- The "Content-Language" meta tag tells search engines what languages your website is available in.

- The "Hreflang" meta tag tells search engines what version of your website to serve up to users in different countries.

- The "Robots" meta tag tells search engines whether they should index your website's content.

5. Keywords

   Different markets will use different keywords to search for your product or service. For example, someone in the United States might search for "shoes," while someone in the United Kingdom might search for "trainers." By doing keyword research, you can make sure you're using the right keywords for each market you're targeting.

6. Local hosting

   If you want your website to appear as a top result in another country's search engine, it is important to use local hosting. This means that your website's server should be located in the country that you are targeting. Using local hosting will help improve your website's loading speed, which is an important ranking factor for all search engines.

7. Search engines

   Each country has its own major search engine, and it's important to take into account the differences between them. For example, Google is the dominant search engine in the United States and Europe, but it doesn't have the same market share in Western Asian countries. In China, for example, Baidu is the dominant search engine. As such, it's important to optimize your website specifically for each country's major search engine.

Google

The majority of the world's Internet population uses Google as their primary search engine, so it is important to consider how to optimize for this platform. Google's algorithms are based on user experience, backlink profile, consistency, and content. In order to rank well on Google, a website must have quality content that is relevant to the user's search query, as well as links from other websites.

Baidu

Baidu is the leading search engine in China. Unlike Google, which relies heavily on links, Baidu's algorithm focuses on the content of a website. In order to optimize for Baidu, it is important to have high-quality content that is relevant to the user's search query. It is also important to have keyword-rich titles and descriptions, as well as H1 tags.

Yandex

Yandex is the leading search engine in Russia. Similar to Baidu, Yandex's algorithm focuses on content rather than links. In order to optimize for Yandex, it is important to have high-quality content that is relevant to the user's search query. It is also important to have keyword-rich titles and descriptions, as well as H1 tags.

Improving Website Design and Content for International Users

It is important to keep in mind that not all countries have the same level of Internet access or infrastructure. In some countries, a website might need to be designed specifically for lower-end devices[1] and slower Internet speeds.[2] Additionally, the content on the website should be tailored for each country's culture and customs.

China

As of 2023, China's Internet population has grown to over one billion, with more than 73% of the population using the Internet.[3] However, Internet speeds can vary greatly depending on the region, with some rural areas still struggling with slower Internet speeds. Therefore, website design and content should be optimized for both high- and low-speed Internet connections. It's also essential to be aware of the cultural differences in content creation, such as color symbolism and imagery, and avoid any taboos that might cause offense.

---

[1] Lower-end devices refer to electronic devices, such as smartphones, tablets, and laptops, that are generally less expensive and have lower specifications and capabilities than high-end or premium devices. Website and app developers need to consider the limitations of lower-end devices in their design and development, to ensure that their products can be accessed and used effectively by a wider range of users.

[2] Slower Internet speeds can have a significant impact on user experience and can make it more difficult to access and use online content and services.

[3] Statista. (2022). *China: number of internet users 2022 | Statista.* [online] Available at www.statista.com/statistics/265140/number-of-internet-users-in-china/ [Accessed Feb. 20, 2023].

United Kingdom

The United Kingdom has one of the highest percentages of broadband users in the world, with over 97% of households having a high-speed connection.[4] However, there are still some areas of the country where broadband speeds are slow. Additionally, UK users are accustomed to seeing websites in both English and Welsh languages. So if you want to reach a UK audience, it is important to have both language options available on your website.

United States

Broadband speeds in the United States are some of the fastest in the world, with an average speed of 22Mbps.[5] However, there are still many areas of the country where Internet speeds are slow. Additionally, American culture is very diverse—which means that tailoring content for a US audience can be tricky. It is important to consider things like regional dialects and cultural sensitivities when creating content for US users.

Monitoring International Search Engine Rankings

If you want to effectively market your product or service on a global scale, it is important to monitor international search engine rankings. This data can be used to improve your targeted content and make sure that your website is visible to potential customers in different countries.

---

[4] Broadband Genie. (2022). *Broadband Statistics: Fibre, Coverage & Speed Stats.* [online] Available at www.broadbandgenie.co.uk/broadband-statistics [Accessed Feb. 20, 2023].

[5] Allconnect. (2022). *New Report States US Has World's 13th Fastest Internet | Allconnect.* [online] Available at www.allconnect.com/blog/us-internet-speeds-globally [Accessed Feb. 20, 2023].

Why Monitor International Search Engine Rankings?

There are a number of reasons why you might want to monitor international search engine rankings. For one, it can give you an idea of how visible your website is in different countries. This data can also be used to improve your targeted content. If you see that your website is ranking highly for certain keywords in one country but not in another, you can adjust your content accordingly.

In addition, monitoring international search engine rankings can help you identify new opportunities for marketing your product or service. For example, if you see that your website is ranking highly for a certain keyword in a country where you don't currently have any customers, that could be an indication that there is interest in your product or service in that country.

How to Use Google Analytics to Monitor International Search Engine Rankings

Google Analytics is a free service from Google that gives you detailed insights into your website's traffic. One of the things it can show you is where your visitors are coming from. This information can be useful for a number of reasons, but for our purposes, we're interested in two things: which countries are sending you the most traffic and how that traffic is distributed across different keywords.

To find this information, log in to Google Analytics and go to the "Geo" report under the "Audience" section. Here, you'll see a map of the world with different countries highlighted. The darker the country is colored, the more traffic it's sending you.

You can also use the "Country" drop-down menu to see a list of countries sorted by the amount of traffic they're sending you. This list can be helpful for quickly identifying which countries are your biggest sources of international traffic.

Once you've identified which countries are sending you the most traffic, it's time to take a closer look at how that traffic is distributed across different keywords. To do this, go to the "Keywords" report under the "Acquisition" section and select "All Traffic" from the drop-down menu. Here, you'll see a list of all the keywords that are driving traffic to your site, sorted by country.

This information can be very valuable when it comes to optimizing your content for international audiences. For example, let's say you sell sporting goods and you notice that a lot of your international traffic is coming from Australia and New Zealand. A quick look at the keyword data reveals that people in these countries are searching for terms like "soccer," "football," and "cricket." This tells you that if you want to capture more search traffic from these markets, you need to produce content that's optimized for these keywords.

Key Takeaways

International SXO is a complex process that requires careful consideration of each country's search engine algorithms, Internet infrastructure, cultural differences, and more. By tailoring your website's structure, design, and content to meet the needs of foreign audiences, you can improve your website's visibility and reach new markets around the world. In this chapter, we discussed five advanced SXO techniques that can help you optimize your website for international search engines.

Some key takeaways from this section include

- International SEO and multilingual SEO are different concepts, and both require different optimization techniques.

- When optimizing a website for international search engines, it is important to consider the website's domain name, country-specific TLDs, HTML language tags, meta tags, keywords, local hosting, and search engines.

- Website design and content should be tailored to meet the needs of each country's Internet infrastructure and cultural differences.

- Monitoring international search engine rankings can help identify new opportunities for marketing your product or service and can also give an idea of how visible your website is in different countries.

- Google Analytics is a useful tool to monitor international search engine rankings, and it can also provide insights into which countries are sending the most traffic and how that traffic is distributed across different keywords.

Generating Demand with SXO

As we've seen, SXO is a powerful tool for improving your website's visibility in search engine results pages. But SXO can also be used to generate demand for your product or service.

Choosing High-Converting Keywords

One way to do this is by creating content that's designed to rank highly for long-tail keywords. Long-tail keywords are specific and often very niche-oriented search terms. They tend to be less competitive than more general keywords, which means they can be easier to rank for. And because they're so specific, they tend to be associated with higher conversion rates.

For example, let's say you sell running shoes. A long-tail keyword like "best women's running shoes for flat feet" is much more likely to convert than a general keyword like "running shoes." The reason is that someone who searches for the latter is probably just starting their research and isn't ready to buy anything yet. But someone who searches for the former is already quite far along in the buying process and is therefore more likely to make a purchase.

How to assess the conversion potential of organic keywords:

1. Long-tail keywords

    One way to assess the conversion potential of an organic keyword is by looking at the length of the keyword. Long-tail keywords are typically three or four words long and are very specific. For example, "bathroom remodel ideas" is a long-tail keyword. These keywords have high conversion potential because they are specific and indicate that the person searching is further along in the buying cycle.

2. High-intent keywords

    Another way to assess the conversion potential of an organic keyword is by looking at the intent behind the keyword. High-intent keywords are those that indicate that the person searching is ready to buy. For example, "buy bathroom vanity" is a high-intent keyword. These keywords have high conversion potential because they show that the person searching is ready to make a purchase.

3. Low-competition keywords

    In addition to looking at the length and intent of a keyword, you also want to look at the competition for that keyword. Keywords with low competition are easier to rank for and will generate more traffic than keywords with high competition. For example, "bathroom remodeling ideas" has low competition, while "bathroom remodel" has high competition. Low-competition keywords have high conversion potential because they are easier to rank for and will generate more traffic.

Creating a Long Landing Page with a Lead Magnet Ranking High in SERP

Another way to generate demand with SXO is by creating a long landing page that's optimized for a specific, high-intent keyword. It should include a lead magnet, an incentive that you offer visitors in exchange for their contact information. It can be anything from an ebook or whitepaper to a discount code or free trial.

The goal of offering a lead magnet is to get visitors to convert into leads, which you can then nurture and eventually turn into customers. Creating a long landing page that's optimized for a high-intent keyword can be an effective way to generate leads from organic search traffic.

How to write a long landing page that will rank well organically:

1. Start with a keyword-optimized headline

   Choose a long-tail keyword that accurately reflects the content of your page and use it in the headline. This will help your page rank fast for that keyword.

2. Make your value proposition clear

   Your value proposition is the main reason why someone should convert on your page. Make sure it's clear and easy to understand.

3. Include a strong call to action (CTA)

    Your CTA should be clear, concise, and persuasive. It should tell visitors what they need to do next and make it easy for them to take action.

4. Use images and videos

    Images and videos can help break up the text on your page and make it more visually appealing. They can also help explain complex concepts more clearly.

5. Optimize your page for SEO

    Make sure you include all the necessary on-page SEO elements, such as title tags, meta descriptions, header tags, etc. This will help your page rank higher in search engine results pages.

6. Use testimonials and social proof to build trust and credibility

    Include testimonials from satisfied customers and social proof (such as customer logos) to show that you're a credible and trustworthy business.

7. Make your page mobile-friendly

    More and more people are using their smartphones to search the Web, so it's important to make sure your page is mobile-friendly. This means having a responsive design that adjusts to different screen sizes.

8. Include a lead capture form

   Make it easy for visitors to convert by including a
   lead capture form on your page. Ask for only the
   essential information (such as name and email
   address) and make the form easy to fill out.

9. Test, measure, and optimize

   Always test your pages before publishing them live.
   Measure your results and optimize your pages based
   on what's working and what's not.

Creating Blog Content to Answer Common Questions

Another great way to generate demand with SXO is by creating blog
content that answers common questions people have about your product
or service. This type of content is often called "top-of-the-funnel" or
"TOFU" content because it's aimed at people who are just starting their
research and are not yet ready to buy anything.

The goal of TOFU content is to attract these early-stage searchers
to your website and get them interested in what you have to offer. Once
you've captured their attention, you can then move them further down the
sales funnel with more targeted content and offers.

How to create TOFU blog content that will rank well organically:

1. Start with keyword research

   Use a tool like Google Keyword Planner or SEMrush
   to find long-tail keywords that people are searching
   for. These keywords should be related to your
   product or service.

209

2. Create content that answers common questions

    Use the keywords you've found to create blog posts
    or other types of content that answer common
    questions people have. Make sure your content is
    well-written and informative.

3. Optimize your pages for SEO

    Include all the necessary on-page SEO elements,
    such as title tags, meta descriptions, header tags,
    etc. This will help your pages rank higher in search
    engine results pages.

4. Promote your content

    Once your content is published, promote it through
    social media, email marketing, and other channels.
    This will help more people find and read your
    articles.

5. Test and measure your results

    Always test your pages before publishing them live.
    Measure your results and optimize your pages based
    on what's working and what's not.

Using Round-Up Blogs to Increase Brand Awareness and Website Traffic

Round-up blogs are a great way to increase brand awareness and website
traffic. They work by featuring other businesses or influencers in your
industry, which can help you get in front of a new audience.

In addition, round-ups tend to be very shareable, so they can generate a lot of social media engagement and word-of-mouth marketing.[6] This can further amplify your reach and help you attract even more visitors to your website.

Here's how to create a successful round-up blog:

1. Choose a topic that will be interesting to your target audience

    Your topic should be something that is relevant to your niche or industry. It should also be something that people would be interested in reading about.

2. Find businesses or influencers to feature

    Reach out to other businesses or influencers in your industry and ask if they would be interested in being featured in your round-up blog. Make sure to choose people who have a large following and are respected in your industry.

3. Create the blog post

    Once you have all the content, put it all together in a blog post. Include a brief introduction, followed by the individual pieces of content. Be sure to link back to each business or influencer's website so people can learn more about them.

---

[6] Word-of-mouth marketing (WOMM) refers to a marketing strategy that relies on the power of personal recommendations and referrals from satisfied customers to promote a product or service. Word-of-mouth marketing can take many forms, including customer reviews, social media shares and posts, testimonials, and direct referrals. The effectiveness of word-of-mouth marketing comes from the trust and credibility that people place in the opinions and experiences of their friends, family members, and peers. By encouraging positive word-of-mouth marketing and providing excellent customer experiences, businesses can generate organic growth and reach new customers through the power of personal recommendations.

4. Optimize your page for SEO

   Include all the necessary on-page SEO elements, such as title tags, meta descriptions, header tags, etc. This will help your pages rank higher in search engine results pages.

5. Promote your blog post

   Once your blog post is published, promote it through social media, email marketing, and other channels. This will help more people find and read your article.

6. Test and measure your results

   Always test your pages before publishing them live. Measure your results and optimize your pages based on what's working and what's not.

Key Takeaways

Utilizing SXO strategies can greatly improve your website's visibility in search engine results pages and can be used to generate demand for your product or service. Choosing high-converting long-tail keywords, creating a long landing page with a lead magnet, creating blog content to answer common questions, and using round-up blogs to increase brand awareness and website traffic are all effective ways to generate demand with SXO.

Some key takeaways from this section include

- Long-tail keywords with high intent and low competition have the highest conversion potential.

- Long landing pages optimized for high-intent keywords with lead magnets can generate more leads from organic search traffic.

- TOFU blog content that answers common questions can attract early-stage searchers and move them further down the sales funnel.

- Round-up blogs featuring other businesses or influencers in your industry can increase brand awareness and generate social media engagement.

- On-page SEO optimization, testing, measuring, and continuous optimization are key components of successful SXO strategies.

AI, Machine Learning, and Automation in SXO

As search engines continue to evolve, they are getting better and better at understanding user intent. This means that businesses need to find new ways to optimize their websites in order to stay ahead of the competition.

One way to do this is through the use of artificial intelligence (AI),[7] machine learning,[8] and automation.[9] These technologies can help you understand how users are interacting with your website and then make changes based on that data.

While this guide's primary audience isn't developers, the following text is a high-level overview of how you could use AI, machine learning, and automation in SXO.

---

[7] Artificial intelligence (AI) refers to the development and use of computer systems and algorithms that can perform tasks that typically require human intelligence, such as visual perception, speech recognition, decision-making, and language translation. AI technology involves the creation of algorithms and models that can learn from data, identify patterns, and make predictions or decisions based on that learning. AI technology has a wide range of applications in many industries and fields, including healthcare, finance, transportation, education, and entertainment. Some of the most commonly used AI technologies today include natural language processing, computer vision, machine learning, and neural networks.

[8] Machine learning is a type of artificial intelligence that involves the development of computer algorithms and models that can learn from data and improve over time without being explicitly programmed. Machine learning models use statistical techniques to identify patterns in data and can then use those patterns to make predictions or decisions. Machine learning has a wide range of applications, such as image and speech recognition, natural language processing, recommendation systems, and predictive modeling. Some common machine learning techniques include supervised learning, unsupervised learning, and reinforcement learning.

[9] Automation refers to the use of technology and computer systems to perform tasks and processes that would otherwise require human intervention or manual labor. Automation can involve the use of software, machines, and robotics to perform a wide range of tasks, such as data entry, manufacturing, customer service, and transportation. The goal of automation is to increase efficiency, reduce costs, and improve accuracy and consistency in the performance of tasks. Automation can also enable the creation of new products and services that were previously not possible and can free up human workers to focus on more creative or complex tasks.

214

Content Creation

Artificial intelligence (AI) can help to improve the quality and relevance of your content, as well as optimize it for better search engine ranking. Google's RankBrain algorithm[10] is already using AI to better understand user queries and deliver more relevant results. And with the recent release of OpenAI's[11] ChatGPT,[12] it's only going to become more common for AI to be used in content writing and SEO. All this means that in order to stay ahead of the competition, businesses need to start using AI in their content marketing and SEO efforts.

---

[10] Google's RankBrain algorithm is an artificial intelligence (AI) system that was introduced in 2015 to help improve the relevance and accuracy of Google search results. RankBrain uses machine learning technology to interpret and understand complex search queries and to provide more relevant and useful search results for users. The algorithm can recognize patterns and relationships between different search queries and can use that knowledge to better understand the intent behind a user's search. RankBrain is one of many factors that Google uses to determine the ranking of search results, and it has become an increasingly important part of Google's search ranking algorithm over time.

[11] OpenAI is an artificial intelligence (AI) research organization that was founded in 2015 by a group of technology leaders, including Elon Musk and Sam Altman. OpenAI's mission is to create advanced AI technologies that are safe, beneficial, and aligned with human values. The organization conducts research in a variety of areas, such as natural language processing, computer vision, robotics, and reinforcement learning. OpenAI also develops and releases AI software and tools, including the GPT language models and the Gym platform for reinforcement learning research. OpenAI has partnerships with many leading technology companies and organizations and is widely recognized as one of the most influential and innovative AI research organizations in the world.

[12] ChatGPT is a large language model created by OpenAI that is designed to provide natural language processing and generation services to users. ChatGPT uses advanced machine learning algorithms and deep learning neural networks to understand and respond to natural language queries and conversations. The model has been trained on a vast amount of data from various sources, including books, articles, and websites, and has the ability to generate human-like responses to a wide range of topics and questions. ChatGPT is widely used in a variety of applications, such as chatbots, customer service, and language translation.

Natural Language Processing (NLP)

NLP is a branch of AI that deals with the interactions between computers and human languages. NLP is used for a variety of tasks, including text classification, information extraction, machine translation, and sentiment analysis. NLP can be used to help content writers create better content by understanding the user's intent and extracting information from unstructured data sources.

How can you use NLP in SXO?

1. Structured data markup automation

   NLP can be used to automatically generate structured data markup for your content. This can help your pages appear in rich search results and also make it easier for search engines to understand your content. In order to classify your text, you can use a tool like the Google Cloud Natural Language API or ChatGPT.

2. Query understanding and intent detection

   Better understanding user queries is crucial for providing relevant results. With NLP, you can analyze user queries to understand the user's intent and match it with the most relevant content on your website. You can again use a tool like the Google Cloud Natural Language API to analyze user queries and extract the entities, keywords, and sentiment. If you have experience in Python, you can also use the Natural Language Toolkit (NLTK).

3. Text summarization

   Text summarization is the process of automatically generating a short summary of a text document. This can be used to create summaries of blog posts, articles, and other pieces of content. Text summarization can be done using a number of different methods, including extractive and abstractive methods.[13]

Extractive methods select the most important sentences from the text and use them to create a summary. Abstractive methods, on the other hand, generate new sentences that capture the meaning of the text.

There are a number of open source libraries and tools that you can use for text summarization, including NLTK, Gensim, Sumy, and Python TextRank.

If you're a beginner, you can instead use widely available tools like Summari—an online tool that uses the TextRank algorithm[14] to generate summaries of texts. The downside is your data will be stored on their servers.

---

[13] Extractive methods involve selecting and combining the most important sentences or phrases from a source text to create a summary. This approach relies on identifying the most relevant information in the source text and presenting it in a condensed form. Extractive methods do not involve generating new text, but instead focus on presenting the most important information from the source. Abstractive methods, on the other hand, involve generating new text that captures the essence of the source text. Abstractive methods use natural language generation techniques to create a summary that is more condensed and easier to understand than the original source. This approach involves using advanced algorithms to understand the meaning and context of the source text and then creating a summary that conveys that meaning in a more concise form.

[14] TextRank is an algorithm used in natural language processing and text summarization to identify the most important sentences or phrases in a piece of text. The algorithm uses a graph-based approach to analyze the relationships between sentences or phrases in the text and identify the most important ones.

4. Keyword and topic modeling

    Keyword and topic modeling are techniques that
    can be used to automatically identify the most
    important keywords and topics in a text. This can
    be used to help content writers create more relevant
    and targeted content that will also rank better in
    SERP for particular terms and topic groups.

There are a number of open source tools[15] that you can use for keyword and topic modeling, including MALLET, Gensim, and scikit-learn. You can also use the Google Cloud Natural Language API.

GPT-3

GPT-3 is the latest generation of language models from OpenAI. It's a neural network[16] that's been trained on a large amount of text data and can be used for a variety of tasks, including text generation, translation, and summarization. While GPT-3 is still in beta, it's already being used by a number of companies, including Microsoft.

---

[15] Open source tools are software programs and applications that are developed and made available to the public for free and whose source code is freely available for anyone to use, modify, and distribute. Open source tools are typically developed by a community of developers and users who collaborate to create software that is useful, reliable, and accessible to everyone. They are used in a wide range of industries and applications, such as web development, data analysis, graphic design, and scientific research. Some popular open source tools include the Linux operating system, the Apache web server, the Python programming language, and the WordPress content management system.

[16] A neural network is a type of machine learning model that is designed to recognize patterns and relationships in data and to make predictions based on that learning. Neural networks are inspired by the structure and function of the human brain and are composed of interconnected nodes, or neurons, that are organized into layers. Neural networks are trained on a large amount of data, and the connections between the neurons are adjusted over time to optimize the model's performance.

1. Machine translation

   GPT-3 can be used for machine translation, which is the process of translating text from one language to another. Machine translation is a difficult task because it requires a deep understanding of grammar and syntax in both languages. However, GPT-3 has been shown to be very effective at translating text, outperforming other machine translation systems in several tests.

2. Generative modeling

   GPT-3 can also be used for generative modeling, which is the process of creating new data based on existing data. The model is trained on a large dataset of data, which are then fed into the model one at a time. The model then generates new data that resembles the existing data.

3. Virtual assistants

   GPT-3 can be used to create virtual assistants that are able to understand and respond to natural language queries. This would allow users to ask questions or give commands to their virtual assistant in a way that is similar to how they would interact with a human being.

4. Chatbots

   GPT-3 can also be used to create chatbots that are able to hold conversations with human beings. This could be used for customer service or other applications where it would be beneficial to have a machine that is able to understand and respond to natural language.

219

DALL-E

DALL-E is a neural network that uses artificial intelligence to generate images from textual descriptions, revealed by OpenAI on January 5, 2021. It uses a 12-billion parameter training version of the GPT-3 transformer model to interpret the natural language inputs and generate corresponding images. DALL-E is capable of creating detailed images from relatively simple text descriptions, even if it has not seen similar text before; for example, it can generate an image of a "pizza with ice cream" even though it has not been trained on a specific combination of these two concepts.

The network has also been used to generate images of more abstract concepts, such as "peace" or "anxiety." While the results are often impressively realistic, they are sometimes surreal or comical, due to the limited understanding of the neural network. Overall, DALL-E represents a significant advance in artificial intelligence and its ability to generate realistic images from textual descriptions.

1. Image generation

   DALL-E is primarily used for image generation from textual descriptions. It's able to interpret the natural language inputs and generate corresponding images. Most businesses use DALL-E for creating mood boards[17] and concept art.[18]

---

[17] A mood board is a visual tool used in design and creative projects to gather and organize ideas, inspirations, and concepts. Mood boards can be created using a variety of tools, such as physical boards, digital collages, or online platforms. They can be used in a wide range of creative projects, such as graphic design, interior design, fashion design, and advertising. Mood boards can help designers to communicate their ideas and concepts to clients, collaborators, or stakeholders and to ensure that the final product meets their expectations and vision.

[18] Concept art is a visual representation of ideas and concepts for various forms of creative media, such as movies, video games, animations, and comics. Concept art is used to explore and develop the visual style and direction of a project and to help communicate and visualize the creative vision of the artist or designer.

2. Abstract conceptualization

    DALL-E is also capable of generating images of more abstract concepts, such as "peace" or "anxiety." This can be used for marketing purposes or to get a better understanding of consumer sentiment.

3. Product design

    DALL-E can be used for product design, as it's able to generate realistic images of products that don't yet exist. This can be used for prototyping or simply for generating ideas.

Scraping Data

By using intelligent algorithms, AI can quickly and efficiently gather data from a wide range of sources, including websites, social media platforms, and online forums. This data can then be used to create detailed buyer personas, track customer sentiment, and identify trends and emerging markets.

In an increasingly competitive landscape, businesses that are able to make use of AI-powered data scraping will have a significant advantage over those that don't.

However, while data scraping[19] can be a useful tool, it is important to use it ethically and responsibly. Gathering data without the consent of the people involved can violate their privacy and lead to legal repercussions. Therefore, it is important to only scrape data from public sources and to ensure that any information used is anonymized.

How can you use data scraping in SXO?

1. Data gathering for market research

    By using specialized software to collect data from online sources such as social media and ecommerce platforms, you can obtain a large amount of data in a relatively short amount of time. This data can then be used to understand trends in consumer behavior, identify potential new markets, and formulate marketing strategies.

    For example, you could use data scraping to gather data on the types of products that are being purchased by consumers in a particular market. This information could then be used to create targeted marketing campaigns or develop new products that meet the needs of this market.

---

[19] Data scraping, also known as web scraping or data harvesting, is the process of extracting data from websites and other online sources. Data scraping involves using software or code to automatically collect and extract data from a website or other online sources, typically in an automated and systematic way. Data scraping can be used for a variety of purposes, such as gathering information for research, monitoring competitors, or collecting data for machine learning and AI models. However, data scraping can also raise ethical and legal concerns, particularly if the data being scraped is private or protected by copyright or intellectual property laws.

You can gather data manually or by using a data scraping tool. If you choose to use a tool, make sure that it is legal and ethical to do so in your country. Typically, ethical scraping tools will default to parameters so that you only collect data that is publicly available and will not violate anyone's privacy. This would include, for example, only scraping data from social media posts that are set to "public" and not "private."

2. Data analysis

    Once you have collected a large amount of data, it's important to analyze it in order to extract valuable insights. This can be done using a variety of methods, such as statistical analysis, data mining,[20] and machine learning.

3. Data-driven decision-making

    One of the most important applications of data scraping is its ability to support data-driven decision-making. In today's business environment, it's essential to make decisions based on data rather than gut feeling.

---

[20] Data mining is a process of extracting and analyzing large and complex datasets to identify patterns, trends, and relationships that can be used to make business decisions or predictions. Data mining involves using advanced algorithms and techniques to uncover hidden insights and relationships in large volumes of data. Data mining can be used for a variety of purposes, such as customer segmentation, fraud detection, market analysis, and predictive modeling. Data mining techniques can also be used in machine learning and AI models to improve accuracy and performance.

By using data scraping to gather accurate and up-to-date information, you can ensure that your decisions are based on solid evidence. This will help you avoid making costly mistakes and will enable you to make decisions that are in the best interests of your business.

Data scraping can be a powerful tool for SXO, but it's important to use it responsibly. Only scrape data from public sources and ensure that any information used is anonymized. This will help you avoid violating anyone's privacy and will ensure that your data gathering activities are legal.

Advanced Pattern Matching with Regex for SXO

Regular expressions (regex) are a powerful tool for matching patterns in strings of text. They can be used for a wide range of tasks, including data validation, data cleansing, and data scraping. In SXO, regex can be used to quickly and efficiently gather data from a wide range of sources.

1. Introduction to regular expressions

   A regular expression (regex) is a sequence of characters that define a search pattern. This search pattern can be used to match character strings in text, which makes them very useful for tasks such as

   – Extracting information from log files

   – Cleaning up data before importing it into a database

   – Validating user input (e.g., email addresses)

   – Finding and replacing text in documents or code files

   The power of regular expressions comes from the ability to specify complex patterns of characters such as repeated occurrences, alternatives, and even backtracking if needed. These possibilities come at the cost of increased complexity compared to using plain text searches. However, once you get familiar with the syntax of regular expressions, they can be very powerful in finding the information you need quickly without having to wade through large amounts of data manually.

Syntax: Characters and metacharacters

A character in regex is any letter, number, or symbol that is not a metacharacter. A metacharacter is any character that has a special meaning in a regular expression. For instance, the period (.) is a metacharacter that matches any single character (except for newline characters).

Some other common metacharacters include

- The asterisk (*), which matches zero or more occurrences of the preceding character

- The plus sign (+), which matches one or more occurrences of the preceding character

- The question mark (?), which matches zero or one occurrence of the preceding character

- The vertical bar (|), which acts as an OR operator

- The backslash (\), which is used to escape special characters

- The caret (^), which matches the beginning of a string

- The dollar sign ($), which matches the end of a string

- The square brackets ([and]), which are used to create character classes

- The parentheses ((and)), which are used to group characters together

- The curly braces ({ and }), which are used to specify the number of occurrences of the preceding character or character class

2. Using regular expressions for data analysis

    Data scraping is one of the most common uses for regular expressions. By using regex, you can quickly and easily extract specific pieces of information from a larger body of text. This can be very useful for tasks such as

    – Collecting data from log files

    – Cleaning up data before importing it into a database

    – Extracting information from web pages

    For instance, let's say you want to extract all the email addresses from a document. You could use the following regular expression:

    \b([A-Z0-9._%+-]+)@([A-Z0-9.-]+)\.[A-Z]{2,}\b

    This regex will match any string that

- Starts with a word boundary (\b)

- Contains one or more characters in the range A–Z, 0–9, or . _ % + - (the square brackets define a character class)

- Is followed by an @ sign

- Contains one or more characters in the range A–Z, 0–9, or . - (again, the square brackets define a character class)

- Is followed by a . (dot)

- Ends with two or more characters in the range A–Z (this is defined by the curly braces { and })

- And is followed by a word boundary (\b)

This regular expression will match any email address, even if it's in the middle of a sentence. For instance, the following text would match our regex:

I can be reached at john.smith@example.com or at 555-123-4567.

Regex can also be used in tools such as Google Analytics to filter data. For instance, you could use a regex to create a filter that only includes pages that contain certain letters or expressions in their URL. This can be very useful for collecting data from a large website with many different pages. For example, if you want to collect data from all pages that discuss cats, you could use a regex filter that searches for any relevant terms, such as "cat," "feline," or "kitten."

Regex can also be used to validate data. For instance, you could use a regular expression to make sure that an email address is entered in the correct format. This can be very useful for preventing errors when collecting data from users.

3. Creating a regular expression

    There are two ways to create a regular expression:

    – With a regular expression generator

    – By writing the regex yourself

    If you're not familiar with regular expressions, or
    if you need to create a complex regex, it's often
    easier to use a regular expression generator. There
    are many different regex generators available
    online, such as RegexBuddy. These tools allow you
    to enter the text that you want to match, and they
    will automatically generate the correct regular
    expression for you.

    If you're familiar with regular expressions, or if you
    only need to create a simple regex, you can write the
    regex yourself.

    When creating a regular expression, there are a few
    things to keep in mind:

    • The characters that you want to match

    • The characters that you don't want to match

    • The position of the match

    • The length of the match

    For instance, let's say you want to match the word
    "cat" in the following text:

    The cat is black.

    You could use the following regular expression:

    \bcat\b

This regex will match the word "cat" if it appears at the beginning or end of a word. So, it would match "cat" in the following text:

- "The cat is black."

- "The dog is black, but the cat is white."

However, it would not match "cat" in the following example:

- "I like both cats and dogs."

4. Testing a regular expression

Once you've created a regular expression, it's important to test it to make sure that it works correctly. You can test a regex by entering it into a regex tester, such as RegexBuddy or Regex101. These tools will allow you to enter some text and see if the regex matches.

It's also a good idea to test your regular expression on a variety of different inputs, to make sure that it works correctly in all cases. For instance, if you're using a regular expression to match email addresses, you should test it with different types of email addresses, such as addresses with different domain names or with different numbers of characters.

5. Using a regular expression

Once you've created and tested a regular expression, you can use it in a variety of different ways.

Regular expressions can be used for

- Searching: You can use a regular expression to search for text that matches a certain pattern. For instance, you could use a regex to search through a document for all email addresses or phone numbers.

- Replacing: You can use a regular expression to replace text that matches a certain pattern. For instance, you could use a regex to replace all instances of the word "cat" with the word "dog."

- Validating: You can use a regular expression to validate data. For instance, you could use a regex to make sure that an email address is entered in the correct format.

Key Takeaways

Artificial intelligence (AI), machine learning, and automation have become essential tools in search experience optimization (SXO). These technologies can help businesses understand user behavior, create targeted content, and gather valuable data. With the continued evolution of search engines, it's important for businesses to stay ahead of the competition by incorporating these technologies into their SXO strategies.

Some key takeaways from this section include

- AI, machine learning, and automation can help businesses optimize their websites for better search engine ranking by improving the quality and relevance of their content.

- Natural language processing (NLP) is a branch of AI that can be used for structured data markup automation, query understanding and intent detection, text summarization, and keyword and topic modeling.

- GPT-3 and DALL-E are powerful tools for text generation, translation, summarization, and image generation from textual descriptions.

- Data scraping can be used for market research, data analysis, and data-driven decision-making, but it's important to use it ethically and responsibly.

- Regular expressions (regex) are a powerful tool for matching patterns in text and can be used for data analysis and cleaning up data before importing it into a database. It can also be used for filtering large volumes of data in popular analytics tool, such as Google Analytics.

Summary

- International and multilingual SEO need different techniques for optimization.

- To optimize for international search engines, consider the website's domain name, country-specific TLDs, HTML language tags, meta tags, keywords, local hosting, and search engines.

- Adapting website design and content to meet the Internet infrastructure and cultural differences of each country is essential.

- Keeping an eye on international search engine rankings can reveal new marketing opportunities and website visibility.

- Google Analytics can provide insights into international search engine rankings and traffic distribution.

- Long-tail keywords with low competition and high intent can boost conversion rates.

- A lengthy landing page that caters to high-intent keywords with a lead magnet can result in more leads from organic search traffic.

- Crafting top-of-the-funnel (TOFU) blog content that addresses common questions can attract early-stage searchers and guide them toward making a purchase.

- Round-up blogs highlighting other businesses or influencers in the industry can enhance brand recognition and social media engagement.

- On-page SEO optimization, testing, measuring, and continuous optimization are fundamental to successful SXO strategies.

- Natural language processing (NLP) can be used for structured data markup automation, query comprehension, and intent detection.

- Scraping data is helpful for conducting market research, data analysis, and making data-driven decisions, but it is important to use it responsibly.

- Regular expressions (regex) are useful for detecting patterns in text and can be employed for data analysis.

CHAPTER 5

The Future of SXO: How It Will Shape the SEO, CRO, and UX Design Landscape

SXO is still in its early stages, but it has already begun to have a major impact on the landscape of SEO, CRO, and UX design. As more and more businesses begin to realize the importance of delivering a great search experience, SXO is likely to become an increasingly important part of the digital marketing mix.

How SXO Will Shape the Future of SEO

The future of SEO is all about personalization. In the past, SEO was all about cramming as many keywords onto a page as possible in order to rank high in Google searches. However, this approach is no longer effective because Google's algorithms have become much more sophisticated. These days, Google takes into account a variety of factors when determining which results to show for a given query.

© Zuzanna Krüger 2023
Z. Krüger, *The Art of SXO*, Design Thinking, https://doi.org/10.1007/978-1-4842-9212-9_5

One of the most important factors is the searcher's intent. Google is constantly working to understand the searcher's intent behind a given query in order to show the most relevant results. This is where SXO comes in.

SXO is all about optimizing the search experience for the user. By understanding what the user is looking for and delivering results that are relevant and helpful, SXO can help to improve the search experience and, as a result, improve SEO.

This means that instead of trying to rank high for generic keywords, you should focus on ranking high for specific queries that are relevant to your target audience and their needs. You should also consider the user journey at each stage of the marketing funnel when choosing your keywords and planning your content strategy.

In the future, SEO will be all about creating a great search experience for the user. And SXO will be a major part of that.

How SXO Will Shape the Future of CRO

In the past, the focus of CRO has been on optimizing individual elements on a page, such as an active voice headline, call to action, or generic pop-ups. As a result, many CRO practitioners have adopted a "test everything" approach in which they test a variety of different elements on the page in an attempt to find the magic combination that will result in more conversions.

However, this approach is no longer effective because it fails to take into account the overall browsing experience. Instead of focusing on individual elements, SXO takes a holistic approach to optimization.

SXO is all about understanding the user's needs and delivering a great search experience that meets those needs. By understanding what the user is looking for and delivering results that are relevant and helpful,

SXO can help to improve the user journey as a whole and, as a result, increase conversions—and not just on your website but also in your overall marketing funnel. In fact, SXO can even help you to identify and fix conversion issues that are not related to the technical state of your website or visual appeal, such as poor customer service or a complicated checkout process.

Creating a great user journey is vital for the success of CRO. And SXO is the key to achieving that.

How SXO Will Shape the Future of UX Design

The future of UX is all about providing an intuitive and seamless experience for users. In today's world, people are used to having instant access to information at their fingertips whenever they want it. They expect websites and apps to be easy to use and understand without any need for instruction. If a website or app is difficult to use or understand, users will simply give up and move on to something else.

SXO can help you create a better UX by allowing you to understand exactly what users are looking for when they visit your site or use your app. By understanding the user's needs, you can design an experience that is tailored to those needs. And by delivering relevant and helpful results, you can keep users engaged and reduce the likelihood that they will give up and go somewhere else.

In the future, UX will be all about understanding the user's needs and delivering a great experience that meets those needs. SXO will play a crucial role in that.

The Bottom Line

Search is constantly evolving. What worked yesterday might not work today. And what works today might not work tomorrow. This is why it's so important to stay up to date with the latest trends and developments in search.

SXO is one of the most important trends in search right now. And it's only going to become more important in the future. If you want to stay ahead of the curve, you need to start implementing SXO into your website and marketing strategy today.

Don't wait. The future of search is happening now. And SXO is leading the way.

Index

© Zuzanna Krüger 2023
Z. Krüger, *The Art of SXO*, Design Thinking, https://doi.org/10.1007/978-1-4842-9212-9

Printed in the United States
by Baker & Taylor Publisher Services